"In *The Limitless School*, Abe and Adam give us, teachers and administrators, the keys to driving our classrooms and schools onto the highway to success! If you want your school culture to exude curiosity, imagination, hope, and love, you must read this book from front to back. Read it twice if you want every teacher, parent, and student in the nation to move to your town to attend your school! Let's go for kids!!"

—**Salome Thomas-EL**, award-winning principal and author

"If you can create a school atmosphere that children want to run into, the sky is the limit in education. In *The Limitless School*, Adam and Abe provide you with nine pillars they believe are essential in creating such an environment. While changing the culture of a school won't happen overnight, this book will provide you with the foundation so you can start the journey today."

—**Ryan McLane**, coauthor of *Your School Rocks . . . So Tell People!*

"In *The Limitless School*, you will find ideas and insights into how you can transform the culture of your school into a school where everyone wants their child to attend. From the S.P.E.C.I.A.L. way to greet someone to the ideas for creating the school mission and vision, the insights, research, and stories Abe and Adam share will empower you to make changes in what you already do and challenge you to become even better. Each section and chapter gave me ideas and real strategies for taking my school to the next level and building a school where students come first and their futures become limitless!"

—**Jay Billy**, principal and author

The

School

CREATIVE WAYS TO SOLVE THE CULTURE PUZZLE

ABE HEGE & ADAM DOVICO

The Limitless School
© 2018 by Abe Hege and Adam Dovico

This book is available at special discounts when purchased in quantity for use as premiums, promotions, fundraisers, or for educational use. For inquiries and details, contact the publisher at books@daveburgessconsulting.com.

Rubik's Cube® used by permission Rubik's Brand Ltd. www.rubiks.com.

Published by Dave Burgess Consulting, Inc.
San Diego, CA
http://daveburgessconsulting.com

Cover Design by Genesis Kohler
Editing and Interior Design by My Writers' Connection

Library of Congress Control Number: 2017961375
Paperback ISBN: 978-1-946444-50-9
Ebook ISBN: 978-1-946444-51-6

Dedication

Adam
To all those who gave me a chance.

Abe
To my wife, Brittany: Your unconditional support for all my crazy ideas is what drives me daily.
To my mentor, Dr. Wheat: For showing me a different way to lead.

Contents

FOREWORD

By Beth Houf, principal and coauthor of *Lead Like a PIRATE*

Recently, a workshop participant came up to me and made a statement I will remember for the rest of my days. Are you ready for it? Because I definitely was not!

"We did that culture thing last year, so I'm looking for another focus for this year."

We did that *culture thing*? Seriously? Throughout my twenty years in the education field, I have become much better at controlling the appearance of my face when people say things I am not expecting to hear, but in this instance, it took me a few seconds to get it together. I let the thought soak in. Although it was a challenge, I worked to presume positive intentions in the statement. It was clear that this young leader hadn't received true training in effective leadership. He didn't know what he didn't know. Our conversation continued, and I was able to provide support and next steps to look at school culture through a different lens.

Culture isn't something you *do* to people; it is the bedrock of any school campus. The moment you walk through the doors, you sense it immediately. The energy of the school either draws you in or makes you feel uncomfortable and unsure of what awaits you. The worst-case scenario is that you want to turn around and leave.

Building a positive school culture must be a continual focus for schools that truly want to be successful. It can't be an afterthought or a random focus when negativity creeps up. Culture first, culture next, culture always!

Can students learn in environments that are negative? Of course. But why would you want that for kids? Why would you want that for your staff? Why would you want that for yourself? Culture trumps everything else in an organization. No matter what terrific structures you have in place, systems you have established, or facilities and resources you have cultivated, the culture drives everything. Period.

Our goal should be to create schools that we are proud to send our own children to each day. This book will help you do just that. Through the pages of *The Limitless School*, Adam and Abe share transformational strategies that they have used in their own careers. The ideas they share will definitely get students, staff, parents, *and* your community running in the doors of your school, not out! The authors' perspectives from the varied roles they have served—including teacher, curriculum facilitator, dean of students, professional development presenter, administrator, professor, community member, and parent—can easily be adapted to any school setting.

You are about to uncover a multitude of ways to shift your school culture as well as the essential "why" for doing so. This book should definitely come with a warning label on the cover because you won't be the same after you finish reading it! Adam and Abe will push your thinking, cause you to reflect deeply on your current practices, and inspire and motivate you to continue to strive for greatness.

Get ready, because the possibilities are truly *limitless*!

INTRODUCTION

There are forty-three quintillion (that's eighteen zeros) combinations for the standard Rubik's® Cube. The official Rubik's Cube website states that if there was one cube scrambled for every permutation, when you lined up the cubes end to end it could cover the earth in 273 layers of cubes! Now picture this. You have just two of these cubes on a table. The one on the left is jumbled up. Colors are mixed everywhere. You pick it up and patiently twist and turn, trying to get each of the six colors on their respective sides. Each side of the cube on the right has one color represented. It is a cube that has been "solved." Hold on to that image.

In the United States, there are more than 13,000 school districts, encompassing over 100,000 public schools, all of which face unique and pressing challenges. In each of these school districts, the teachers, students, administrators, families, community, and board members are asked to solve problems every day—often in a very short amount of time.

The visual of the jumbled cube with different colors on each side represents what schools and school leaders deal with on a daily basis: mismatched visions, twisted communications, and overemphasis on menial issues. The other cube is the result of order, patience, strategy, and skill—organization and understanding among all stakeholders.

Sounds great, but how do we get there?

Schools are complex machines. Hundreds of moving parts simultaneously function together to create a place where students are (hopefully) excited to come each day, where teachers and administrators provide high-quality education, where parents advocate for their children, and where the community celebrates the school's efforts and achievements. When these many parts do not work together, conflict arises. This happens all the time. Parents get angry because they did not know their child was failing. A local business is eager to support a school but doesn't know how to or with whom to connect in order to make it happen. The superintendent announces a district-wide program to address struggling readers, but the gifted students haven't shown any growth in years.

We use the Rubik's Cube as a metaphor for the issues today's schools face: There are any number of ways to solve the complex puzzle. With a Rubik's Cube, players twist the sides, looking to align the colors. Sometimes they get lucky, but most of the time, skills and strategy solve the puzzle. In talking with people who have solved the Rubik's Cube (since neither of your authors know how), it became apparent that it is impossible to untangle the mix of colors by looking at the cube's individual colored squares. You must be strategic and deliberate in your moves and recognize the interconnectedness of the sides and pieces.

Schools function on a similar approach. There are any number of ways to "solve" the challenges schools face, and many people have attempted to tackle the issues by looking at the role of the teacher, the parent, the administrator, and so on. But rarely do stakeholders look at the individual parts that comprise school communities as one interconnected entity.

This book attempts to do just that. Through our collective experiences as a teacher, curriculum facilitator, dean of students, professional development presenter, administrator, professor, community member, and parent, we will aim to demonstrate how schools can create an empowering culture when all stakeholders work in harmony. Ultimately, the goal is to create a *Limitless School*, one in which each stakeholder believes that the possibilities for where your school's culture can head are endless, and the only limitations are those you set upon yourself. We truly believe that this can be done when the right adults are put together for a collective goal. Call us optimistic, call us dreamers, but hear our story and you might see why.

* * *

We first met in 2013, when a new public middle school in High Point, North Carolina, Allen Jay Middle School, was being created. At the time, Adam was working for the Ron Clark Academy, a renowned middle school in Atlanta, which also doubles as a teacher-training facility. In addition to teaching, he served as the implementation specialist, which allowed him to travel across the country to help schools bring in innovative strategies. Abe was one of the first four teachers at Allen Jay, which began with just a fifth grade. At the helm of this school was an energetic and innovative principal, Kevin Wheat. Dr. Wheat truly believed the sky was the limit when it came to this school. His dream was that innovation, creativity, and an unparalleled culture would drive Allen Jay Middle School to be successful. His target audience included students who had struggled in their traditional settings and were looking for a different approach toward learning.

While traveling across the country, it became apparent to Adam that many of the schools for which he conducted professional development training were looking to change their culture. The reasons varied: a new principal, a negative staff, frustrated parents and community, failing grades that the board of education wanted to improve, and so on. During these school visits, Adam brought in strategies and ideas from places he had been that were working. He noticed that the schools that were most successful in creating a positive school culture were those where a common message, consistency of innovative practice, and risk-taking were prevalent.

Meanwhile, in High Point, Allen Jay Middle School was building a model school culture. Adam continued to visit Allen Jay, and each time, he noticed different ways that its culture made the school special and unique. He observed that teachers, staff, and administration spoke a common language; students, parents, and guests in the school bought into the excitement and love that permeated the school. He began bringing the strategies of this small middle school to the places he visited.

On the inside, Abe played a central role in creating the culture on which Allen Jay's staff and students prided themselves. When Abe was brought on board in 2013, Dr. Wheat sat down with him and five other staff members to plan out what Allen Jay Middle School would look like and what opportunities it would provide to scholars daily. The main purpose, revealed when determining the vision of the school, hinged on creating a culture where kids wanted to be and where they thrived academically and socially.

Abe and Adam continued chatting over the years about their respective experiences, frequently coming back to core tenets that were working either at Allen Jay or, in particular, schools Adam visited. Those main points, they discovered, became essential to creating a *Limitless School*.

WHAT IS A LIMITLESS SCHOOL?

When coming up with what a limitless school encompasses, we studied the school cultures we have worked in, read about, and researched. We also identified what we believe to be effective strategies within our educational philosophy. What we came up with are nine pillars for what these schools and districts possess. To be a limitless school, all stakeholders must believe in and practice these tenets on a consistent basis; for example, the principal who has a school vision must share it with teachers and parents, who then uphold it in their classrooms and homes. The board of education that wants to create a district of limitless schools finds community support and strong administrators who carry out its calls for action.

What follows is a brief overview of each of the nine pillars that are discussed in the chapters of this book. Your school may already practice some of these pillars. That's fantastic! But a limitless school always looks for ways to be even stronger. Use the examples and concepts in each chapter to inspire your school to experiment and take risks that contribute to strengthening school culture. Our hope is that every school becomes limitless, with the vision, actions, and words to demonstrate unlimited potential and amazing culture each day.

LEADERSHIP

Is the next great leader sitting in your classroom? How do we cultivate and grow leadership skills from *all* stakeholders? The first step is to believe that each individual can be a leader. When you foster a culture of leadership in a school, students and adults alike see themselves as having leadership potential, and instilling that belief is half the battle. Leadership does not have one defined look. When the National Center for Fathering recognized a deficit of male role models in schools, they created Dads of Great Students (Watch D.O.G.S.), which provides positive male role models in schools. These fathers, grandfathers, uncles, and other father-like figures are empowered to demonstrate leadership simply by being present. Their presence helps enhance security, reduce bullying, and encourages positive behavior in students. And they themselves grow as leaders by mentoring students in the school.

Impressions

How many times a day do you walk down the street, hallway, or grocery aisle with your head down, hoping to avoid eye contact with another person? As your head was down, how many people walked by you with a smile? And when they walked by you with that smile, how must they have felt when you continued to keep your head down? We are judged almost instantaneously by individuals based on the impression that we make. In the school setting, first impressions can be the reason why a school gets a positive or negative review, a generous donor, or a new family to move to the district. Unfortunately, how to make a positive first impression is not typically taught in school or the community, until now! Making a S.P.E.C.I.A.L. first impression will change the way that your school interacts with stakeholders and provides a welcoming culture.

Marriage

What qualities do you value in a healthy marriage? Perhaps communication? Compromise? Support? And when things break down in a relationship, isn't it the lack of practicing these values that is so often the heart of the problems? A successful or tumultuous marriage between stakeholders within a school boils down to the same ideals as spouses. To build a positive school culture, we need to respect and understand school stakeholders as our significant others. That doesn't mean we always have to agree with our significant other; there may be moments when we don't even like them. But when push comes to shove, you are partners, and you know you would do anything to protect each other.

Integrity

Being rich, well-connected, or smart may open a few doors for you, but your character and morals are what keep you in the room. A school culture built with integrity maintains transparency and allows stakeholders to trust one another. And it is that trust that prompts stakeholders to take risks—risks that make students excited to come to school and parents eager to have their children at the school. A culture of integrity means that when your back is turned, you don't have to fear what is being said. When someone makes a mistake, the first question is not, "Why would you do that?" but "What can we do to help you fix it?"

TIME

Our society is accustomed to instant gratification. When we have a question, we ask Siri or Alexa and get an immediate answer. If we want to watch a television show that isn't broadcasting at the moment, we press the OnDemand button. There's not much of a need to "wait" anymore for the basic interests in life. That's why it can be difficult for schools to plan for cultural change. Superintendents devise three-year strategic plans, but the reality is that people will start questioning effectiveness after year one if the plan doesn't execute perfectly. Students are supposed to show a year's growth on state assessments, but when they aren't "there yet" in December, we start panicking. For school culture to show improvement and change, leaders and stakeholders need to respect the amount of time necessary to make it happen.

LIMELIGHT

Before the creation of electrical lights, theaters and music halls used to use a cylinder of calcium oxide (quicklime) and an oxyhydrogen flame to create an intense illumination on stage. Though the use of calcium oxide for lighting has long ceased, the term *limelight* remains and refers to someone or something in the public eye. The intense illumination of something piques people's natural curiosity. Why else do cameras whip out when people hear that a celebrity is in the room or when they approach a national monument? We are a society obsessed with the ideals of greatness. What if we were to create a limelight on our schools? What if our schools were seen as a beacon of greatness in the public eye? Imagine a school culture where teachers are seen as celebrities, students are rock stars, and where people whip out their cameras when they enter your school because it exhibits the ideals of excellence.

EDUCATE YOURSELF

We're not just talking about the ABCs and 123s kind of education. Do conversations about race, culture, and privilege occur in your school? Without this dialogue, we're losing out on valuable learning experiences about one another. Our schools and communities become more diverse, but our teaching force is not. This reality requires that we all intentionally improve our cultural competencies so we can build a positive, inviting culture for all stakeholders. It is imperative that we have open and honest discussions about pressing sociological topics so that acceptance is the prevailing sentiment across the school.

SUCCESS

So maybe you *think* you've built a strong leadership structure within your school; you have a feeling that there are healthy marriages going on, and you believe your school is moving into the limelight. But how do you know for sure? How do you measure the success of solving your school's culture cube? Unfortunately, there's not a test score or letter grade that will officially tell you how you're doing, but there are certainly indicators that will let you know whether you're on the right track. And it's important to remember that, even when you make a bad twist or turn on your cube, there's always a way to fix it.

SET GOALS

No school with an organized culture cube got there by simply guessing their way to success. They established short- and long-term goals and watched to see what moves worked and which ones needed adjusting. And what happens when you don't reach your goal on the first try? Ask Thomas Edison, who racked up 10,000 failed attempts at creating the light bulb before inventing one that worked. Or consider Henry Ford, who went bankrupt five times before he made it. Goals give us something to work toward. When you truly want something, you should be willing to work for it. And when you're willing to work for a limitless school, establishing goals will help you get there.

Improving school culture is not easy. Frankly, it's downright frustrating at times, especially when stakeholders don't communicate well or share a common vision. Much like the Rubik's Cube, it's easy to give up and quit trying to solve the problems. That's why we need to celebrate small victories along the way. When you finally get a few colors aligned, celebrate. When you find that each of the stakeholder groups have a common understanding of a pillar, celebrate. And when you are at the point in solving the cube where those who were resistant want to join in, celebrate even harder!

Even when you reach your goals, solving this puzzle we will call the "culture cube" does not mean your school's journey is done! Rather, it means that you have the pieces in place to move even further ahead. The stakeholders in a limitless school continually strive to better themselves, looking for new ways to cultivate a positive culture and engage every member in the effort to help students succeed. The journey is not always smooth and is frequently filled with misses, but it's the wonder of possibility that keeps dreams alive. We hope you dream big with us as we travel into *The Limitless School*.

1

LEADERSHIP

M any years ago, a humble, ambitious eight-year-old student from a loving, close-knit family lost her father. His death, sudden and tragic, shook the little girl's world. In their grief, she and her two siblings grew closer to their mother, a hard-working and spiritual woman. The young girl found interest and comfort in the ability to help others and was supported by her mother, teachers, and community. In fact, it was not uncommon for her family to host dinners for those less fortunate in the community, even though her family was by no means wealthy. Then at age twelve, after an inspiring field trip, she decided to dedicate the rest of her life to charity and helping those less fortunate.

Her name was Anjezë Bojaxhiu, but you may know her as Mother Teresa. While the world knows the impact she made on society as an adult, it is interesting to look at how she became the person who left such a powerful legacy. Had her mother not been a selfless and charitable woman, would Anjezë have grown up to do what she did? Without teachers and community members to guide and provide opportunities for her to see how those less fortunate suffer, would she have grown up to dedicate her life to helping those in need?

Or what about the thirteen-year-old young man who became the youngest assistant manager for a newspaper delivery station in the city? During this time, the young man excelled as a public speaker and was part of the school's debate team. With an already academically and socially successful teenage life, the young man did the unthinkable by skipping the ninth and twelfth grades in high school with the support of his teachers and parents. This helped him enter college at the age of fifteen and graduate at age nineteen. The young man was driven, articulate, passionate, and motivated to do great things.

This student's name was Martin Luther King, Jr. While his academic success was impressive, the fact that it came during a time of racial tension and discrimination in the country makes it even more remarkable. For King to achieve what he did during that time shows the importance and the impact of support he received from those who believed in him and guided him along the way. What if the newspaper company had balked at the idea of a thirteen-year-old taking on a leadership role in the business? What if his parents had squashed his drive for education at an early age? Would he have been the person we still talk about decades later as one of the greatest leaders of all time?

The point here is that you never truly know the potential of the students sitting in your classroom. At the Ron Clark Academy, where Adam worked for a number of years, the teachers are guided in their interactions with their students by one of Ron's mantras: "One of these kids is going to be the President of the United States. We don't know who it's going to be, though, so we'd better prepare all of them to have the job!"

When stakeholders share the mindset that every student holds the potential to be great, our school culture shifts from teaching children to building leaders. When we collectively aim to build leaders, we begin seeing students not as a number or statistic, but as a future Mother Teresa, Martin Luther King Jr., Bill Gates, or Barack Obama.

Building a culture of leadership in schools is exhausting. Kids are kids; they will mess up. When you pour your time, energy, and soul into building positive qualities, and they let you down, it can be frustrating. But then there are moments where you see the true potential of the individual shine, when your students do something remarkable and show you "they *can* do it." When that happens, capture that feeling of unlimited possibility and find ways to replicate it! As teachers, administrators, parents, board of education members, and community members, we must provide opportunities for our students to shine. Even when they don't meet our expectations, we must continue to push them by setting the bar high and supporting them as they strive to reach it. Most importantly, we must show them we believe in them by continuing to give them opportunities to excel.

In addition to a persistent belief in students, modeling is a key to building a culture of leadership. Just like we model how to solve a math problem, how to shoot a basketball, or how to operate a computer program, leadership must be modeled everywhere. It needs to be woven into every part of our schools, our homes, and our community. It needs to be visible and concrete, so that the *concept* of leadership becomes the *practice* of leadership.

> "A genuine leader is not a searcher for consensus but a molder of consensus."
>
> MARTIN LUTHER KING JR., AMERICAN CIVIL RIGHTS LEADER AND ACTIVIST

Most of all, leadership needs to be recognized so that when the eight-year-old girl in the class shows an interest in helping those in need, she has the kind of support that fosters her drive to make a difference in the world.

Through listening and forming relationships with students, adults uncover strengths and weaknesses, providing opportunities for children to grow in their weaknesses and thrive in their strengths. Recognizing leadership qualities early gives students a chance to build confidence and be contributing members in the success of the school.

We recognize how simple this sounds, and we understand the challenge presented by the realities of the school day. We have found a few successful ways to make time to build relationships and discover leadership, include eating lunch with a small group of students, participating

"The most dangerous leadership myth is that leaders are born, that there is a genetic factor to leadership. This myth asserts that people simply either have certain charismatic qualities or not. That's nonsense; in fact, the opposite is true. Leaders are made rather than born."

WARREN BENNIS, AMERICAN SCHOLAR AND ORGANIZATIONAL CONSULTANT in field trips and non-classroom activities, and going to students' out-side-of-school events and performances.

I (Adam) had the opportunity to coach an award-winning Model United Nations team at the Ron Clark Academy. We would continually win recognitions at domestic and international competitions, even when we were the only middle school in a high school competition. As it came time for tryouts one year, I approached one of my top scholars, Alexis, about the team. Alexis was a straight-A student. She worked hard and was a model student, but truthfully, she flew under the radar. She was quiet and reserved, but I saw a fire hiding in there that needed to be exposed. She had leadership potential written all over her, and I wasn't going to let that pass under my watch.

Long story short, she made the team. To help bring out that hidden tiger, my fellow coach and I paired her up with our team captain for competition so that she could see a model of what we knew she could be. We also worked tirelessly on being bold, providing feedback on how to sharpen her diplomatic skills. Alexis would later go on to conduct speeches in front of hundreds of people, become captain of several academic and performance teams, and currently attends an elite college. She's a special young lady.

I have no doubt Alexis was going to be successful with or without us in her life. In talking to her dad years later, however, he said that trying out for Model United Nations and discovering her own leadership potential were the turning points that helped her grow in confidence and break out of the shell that was keeping her from reaching her full potential.

Look around your school; who is your Anjezë, Martin, or Alexis? What are you doing to provide them with the support and guidance needed to be a leader?

PUT LEADERSHIP ON DISPLAY

An important component of teaching leadership and growing a school culture toward leadership is to showcase the leaders you want students and adults to emulate. Inside every school building are hallways, classrooms, and sometimes staircases. Instead of viewing these as the pieces that physically make up the building, we need to look at them as canvases upon which we can showcase leadership; for example, many schools have a main hallway that most students will see at some point during the school day. Throughout the hustle and bustle of class changes, this hallway or commons area can represent the single most important area in your school. At Allen Jay Middle School, one hallway connects

all grade levels to the cafeteria. Students pass down this hallway at least four times every day. When thinking of ways to build the culture of the school, our team named this main thoroughfare *Leadership Lane.*

When walking down Leadership Lane at Allen Jay, you will see murals painted by a local artist that depict Harriet Tubman, Allen Jay, Abraham Lincoln, Rosa Parks, Martin Luther King, Jr., Gandhi, Mother Teresa, and Steven Covey. Around the paintings are quotes from local and world leaders that give insight on ways to encourage the people around you.

Visually, we have provided something for students to look at that is a pathway to success. Each day, the students will look directly at one or more of the paintings or read one of the quotes. We want our students to always be subconsciously thinking of ways to react to situations, both socially and academically, and to grow their leadership philosophy. What better way than by giving them a blueprint of people who have paved the way before them?

Leadership Lane is an effective school culture indicator. It reflects our beliefs and desires regarding behavior and citizenship in a way that provides talking points for teachers, administrators, and students when we have guests in the building. When visitors come to Allen Jay, Leadership Lane is one of their biggest takeaways, not just because it is visually appealing, but because our scholars and staff communicate its purpose and how it ties into the overall vision of the school.

TEACH STUDENTS TO LEAD

For some students, leadership potential does not become realized until their strengths are revealed in a group or organization. Oftentimes, these are hidden strengths that have simply not had the chance to be put to the test yet. As adults, we can lay the foundation for students to grow leadership in group settings by creating experiences to hone in on leadership traits such as working as a team member, bringing people together, supporting others, goal setting, or vision building. Student organizations and groups are an excellent way to help shape and inspire personal leadership in kids by giving them unique opportunities to stretch and share their skills with others to achieve a common goal.

READING BUDDIES (ABE[1])

In 2012, I was looking for something new to do with a group of my students who needed extra academic practice. Standard tutoring just wasn't doing the trick; I needed to get them excited about reading and thought getting them off campus would help. Planning trips to take students off campus can pose challenges, such as parent and administrative approval, transportation, funding, and available time. Everyone has to be on board to make these types of opportunities happen!

My vision was simple: I wanted to give my students extra reading practice while serving in the community at the same time. The first step was to go to the principal to see if she thought my idea could work. I set up a meeting so I could explain what I wanted to do. She was supportive of my plan and gave me a few ideas to move forward. One of her ideas was to collaborate with a local community center.

After our meeting, I went back to my classroom and immediately began looking for a community center to contact. I stumbled upon a resident facility that provided care for less fortunate elderly people. The website noted a need for volunteers, so I emailed the group home advisor, Lee. In my email, I explained that I had a group of students who were looking to engage in the community and build their reading skills at the same time. It was a long shot, but I thought, *Why not try?* Within a few hours, Lee called me, and we talked about the entire process. I told him that I had eight students who were eager to get off campus and serve. He replied that he had eight residents who would love the company of middle school students! We put together

---

1 For parts in the book where either Adam or Abe are telling a personal story, we will include our name with the heading.

the idea and called it the "Reading Buddies Program."

Unfortunately, we did not have enough money to obtain a bus for such a small number of students. I reached out to the parents and told them what we were doing and how I wanted them to be involved if they had any extra time to spare. The response was overwhelming. Not only did the parents want to be involved with the program, they offered to provide a carpool for the eight students to and from the facility.

My students were so excited to go on the first after-school trip. When we arrived, my students jumped right in, introducing themselves and selecting a resident as their partner. From then on, during every visit, the students read to the residents and spent the last twenty minutes of each session asking the residents questions about their lives. The rides back from each outing were the best; the students could not stop talking about how much fun they had reading and listening to the residents. The interactions made the students feel as if they were a part of something bigger than themselves.

As the weeks went on, I wanted to shine a light on my students and the good things they were doing with the Reading Buddies Program. I reached out to the local news station, explaining what we were doing, and let them know how awesome it would be if they would do a report on the students. A few weeks went by, and I didn't hear from the news station. Then, on our final visit at the community center, we walked into something special. When we entered the building, news cameras, a reporter, and a board member from

> "If your actions inspire others to dream more, learn more, do more, and become more, you are a leader."
>
> JOHN QUINCY ADAMS, PRESIDENT OF THE UNITED STATES OF AMERICA

our district were waiting for us. My students were on cloud nine! Here they were, middle schoolers, being interviewed by the local news and getting to share all about the Reading Buddies Program.

As the year came to a close, my students participated in state testing. The scores of the eight students who had participated in the Reading Buddies Program improved tremendously in reading, and five out of the eight students moved to proficient in reading. They always had the skills to be successful; they just needed the right motivation to pull it out and showcase it!

By the end of Reading Buddies, Bill was able to hold a conversation with an adult, Destiny learned how to take critiques in her writing from her buddy and not get frustrated, and Rae learned how to use her soft-spoken tone to support the vision of the group by keeping everyone focused and on time. Individually, these students were given a means for cultivating their leadership qualities and strengths in this group setting, Collectively, these individual efforts moved the group toward reaching their overall goals.

When realizing individual strengths and harnessing them in a group setting, new leadership qualities are being transferred to the school setting, building a stronger culture of student leadership. In return, adult stakeholders are blessed to witness young minds take ownership of their learning and surroundings. The result is students who are proud of their school, excited to be a part of a place that allows them to be leaders.

PHI DELTA (ADAM)

In college, I was what my wife likes to call (in a disenchanted voice) a "frat boy." Her negative perception of fraternities has been shaped by movies like *Animal House* or *Old School*. Fair enough. Movie antics aside, there are many positive attributes to being in a Greek organization. A few of those positives include having male friends whom you can depend on and trust, having opportunities to give back to the community, and learning from mentors and older brothers. These organizations have contributed to an honored tradition in our country from which many men and women have benefited.

While working as a college professor, I volunteered at a middle school that was struggling with eighth-grade behavior. Having benefited from being in a fraternity myself, I decided to create a middle school fraternity that would focus on positive character building with an emphasis on leadership. Working with a staff member at the middle school, we identified twenty-five students for whom this group might be helpful and got permission for them to join. I also applied for and received a small grant that allowed me to purchase ties and white button-down shirts so that the young men could "dress for success."

I scoured the internet for Greek letter symbology to create a name for the group and came across the letters *phi* and *delta*. *Phi* has been interpreted as meaning "light" and *delta* as a "power or force that creates." Working with these loose interpretations of the letters, I explained to the students that, individually, they were beams of light—a small quantity of force—but that collectively they could create great change. Sounds cheesy, but they bought into it, and it became our mantra from then on.

Each month, the group met and took part in activities that instilled positive leadership skills. Because studies show that exposure to college students or a college campus at a young age increases likelihood of attending college, I brought in the Wake Forest University baseball

> "Everyone who's ever taken a shower has an idea. It's the person who gets out of the shower, dries off, and does something about it who makes a difference."
>
> ———————————
>
> NOLAN BUSHNELL, AMERICAN ELECTRICAL ENGINEER

team who taught the young men how to tie a tie, shake hands, and hold conversations.[2] And I invited brothers of the Wake Forest University Alpha Phi Alpha fraternity to join us to teach the boys how to step (a rhythmic combination of footsteps, spoken word, and clapping). I also partnered with the adjacent elementary school's kindergarten class to do a reading program where the middle schoolers read with kindergartner buddies.

Leadership is not simply an action; it's also a mindset. By the end of the school year, these young men felt better about themselves, and their teachers and peers treated them differently. Positive interactions, sincere greetings, and casual conversations took the place of bickering and profanity in many situations. Because these young men began viewing themselves as leaders, so did the rest of the school.

MOD Squad and LOVE Club (Abe)

Giving students and stakeholders the opportunities to teach, model, and practice leadership is invaluable. Much like Adam's Phi Delta, at Allen Jay, a club called Men of Distinction (better known as the MOD Squad) allows the boys of Allen Jay to participate in male-driven leadership opportunities to help foster and develop their growth as leaders in the school, community, and (hopefully) eventually the nation! A similar group called the Ladies of Value and Excellence (LOVE Club for short) gives the young ladies of Allen Jay the same opportunities and leadership qualities and practices from the female staff members.

These clubs focus on serving and engaging the community along with teaching soft skills that the students will need to be successful in life. Both the MOD Squad and LOVE Club are run solely by the staff members of Allen Jay. The teachers who participate are then given three to four mentees with whom they will work throughout the year. Involving teachers to lead these

---

2 Villavicencio, A., Bhattacharya, D., and Guidry, B., July 2013. "Moving the Needle: Exploring Key Levers to Boost College Readiness Among Black and Latino Males in NYC," New York University, Research Alliance for New York City Schools, ERIC, https://eric.ed.gov/?id=ED543855, accessed 19 November 2017.

clubs gives staff the opportunity to build their own teacher-leadership skills and contributes to a more empowered school culture.

Both clubs do a great job of partnering with parents and community members. For starters, anytime a service-learning project or fundraiser is formulated, the students are the ones who call the relevant business or community organization to make arrangements. This responsibility gives the students ownership and builds a culture of proactive leadership.

The LOVE Club has an ongoing partnership with the Special Olympics because three student members called and offered to serve at one of the events. The organization was so impressed with the girls who called that they gave the entire LOVE Club an invitation. For the past two years, more than twenty-five girls have had the opportunity to spend a full day serving at the Special Olympics.

The MOD Squad boys have an ongoing partnership with a local soup kitchen. One day, a young man asked his teacher mentor if he could call the local chapter of the Salvation Army to find ways to serve. With the teacher's guidance and direction, the young man set up the logistics for fifteen of our boys to serve at a soup kitchen.

Through these clubs, the boys and girls have been able to meet and interact with the superintendent, board members, high-ranking public officials, community members, and parents from all over the district. While meeting with diverse groups of people and giving back to the community, the students have learned leadership qualities that have translated into a stronger culture inside the school.

BE AN UPSTANDER

A young man is wandering aimlessly around a park, clearly upset, calling for help without using the words. There's a crowd of people going about their business in the park, but the man's actions catch their attention. Several bystanders begin pulling out their phones and swiping right to quickly turn to video mode so they can record this man acting strangely. What the people recording him don't know is that he is autistic, and he wandered away from his home and is now lost.

The scene, which will likely turn into a Facebook or YouTube video for thousands to share, depicts the grim reality of our society's automatic reaction: record first, act second. Rather than standing idly by watching potentially dangerous or life-changing things happen, our desire is for students and educators to be *upstanders*. Think about what it would take to be an "upstander" in the situation described above. Would it mean approaching the lost young man and asking what was wrong or calling the police to assist the young man if his safety was at risk?

Leadership sometimes requires us to go against the grain, to do something that the rest of the crowd isn't doing. An upstander thinks about how to make the change and then acts upon it. Remember, leadership isn't just about what you say; it's about what you do. In the Watch D.O.G.S. program discussed in the Introduction, men recognized a need in their community, and they acted to fill that need by making time to be present in their child's school. As you consider ways to model leadership for your staff, students, and even your own children, consider the ways that stakeholders can be upstanders in the context of schooling:

- Join the parent teacher association/organization (PTA/PTO) and attend its events and meetings. In our experience, there are a handful of consistent and reliable faces at PTA functions, but the success of a PTA relies on more than the same few people. A successful PTA greatly impacts school culture by providing resources and opportunities for students and staff. If your school does not have a strong PTA, talk to the principal and discuss ways to build one.

- Schools at all levels look for volunteers to assist with various needs. Elementary and middle schools consistently look for reading or lunchtime buddies. We have seen businesses that even work this into their community outreach initiatives. If you're not sure how to get involved, simply call your local school and explain that you want to volunteer. High schools frequently seek out mentors and internship opportunities for their students. If you are in a profession or job that allows interns or shadowing opportunities, reach out to the school and explain that you would be happy to work with students who might be interested in learning more about your career.

- If you are a board member, be visible in your schools and find ways to support your teachers and administrators. One of my (Adam) favorite people is Carolyn Edwards, a trustee of the board for the Clark County School System, which is the fifth-largest district in the United States. Every time I have gone to Las Vegas to conduct professional development at one of Carolyn's schools, she has been there the *entire* day and participates in every single thing the teachers and students do! She knows teachers and students by name and shows leadership by being an active part of the culture of her school district.

The great thing about leadership is that there is no one right way to do it. Pick up any number of books featuring great leaders, and you'll notice that each one has (or had) his or her unique approach to leading. The common thread of great leaders, though, is that they all impact others in positive ways. And in a *limitless school*, the goal is for stakeholders to leave not just a positive mark, but a lasting imprint on the hearts and minds of those they touch.

Creating leaders in our schools involves modeling the qualities we wish to see from others. Be the leader you wish to build.

ABE & ADAM

2

IMPRESSIONS

The nurse at your child's middle school calls and says your sixth-grade son is sick and needs to be picked up. It's been months since you've stepped inside the school. You pull up, walk into the office, and . . . .

Let's pause here for a second. We want you to think about your experiences walking into places like restaurants, businesses, or retail stores. What is your expectation when you walk into one of these places? How do you expect to be greeted by the employees?

Personally, we feel that you should be welcomed with a warm smile, a "hello," and perhaps an inquiry as to how the business can help you. Parents and community members, do you hold those same expectations when you walk into a school? Teachers and administrators, do you have those expectations for your school?

Okay, back to picking up your child. This could go a few ways:

The front office person happily greets you and willingly locates your child so he can go home.

The front office person offers a conventional hello and asks what you need. When you explain that you are picking up your child, they point you to the nurse's office.

The front office person looks up at you, clearly irritated by your presence, and waits for you to say something. They seem inconvenienced that they need to help you.

Whatever the front office person's response is, you, the parent, immediately form a picture in your head of the school's culture based on your encounter in the office.

It's a natural human response to make judgments on places we go based on our experiences. And with technology today, we can easily report our thoughts using review platforms like Yelp, Google, Facebook, and so on. And those reviews aren't just for restaurants and hotels. It is not uncommon for parents and community members to evaluate and "shop" for schools based upon online testimonials and reviews.

The judgments people make about our schools, based on the simplest of encounters, impact the community's perception of the school as well as enrollment and partnerships with local businesses and organizations. When schools have a "good" reputation for being welcoming and warm to students, families, and community members, the student population tends to grow as families decide to live in that area so their child can go to that school. A positive reputation also entices experienced and highly qualified teachers who want to work at schools with the best reputations (and that doesn't just mean those with the highest test scores). Vice versa, a school with a "bad" reputation may suffer with low enrollment, high staff and student turnover, and lack of support from the surrounding community.

Why does this all matter? If we are trying to get *all* schools to have academic success, quality teachers, a vibrant community, and parent support, then the way people perceive our schools is paramount because those perceptions play into whether or not we achieve those goals.

How then do you create positive perceptions of your school? Here are a few ideas:

"You cannot shake hands with a clenched fist."

INDIRA GANDHI, INDIAN STATESWOMAN

THE TYPEWRITER LADY (ADAM)

When I walked into the front office of a school in Virginia where I was presenting a professional development day, an elderly woman looked up at me from behind a typewriter (yes, I said a typewriter). She slowly got up out of her seat, came around her desk (which made me curious and nervous all at the same time) and took my hand in hers. Then, in the most charming Southern accent, she said, "Welcome suga', I'm Ms. Doris, and how can I help you today?" Ms. Doris's smile lit up the room and made me feel like I was part of that school's family already.

While I waited for the principal, Ms. Doris offered me a bottle of water and told me a little about the school. I later found out that Ms. Doris has been at the school for more than fifty years! And yes, she still uses the typewriter. She has seen generations upon generations walk through the school's doors, and I believe it's that warm greeting that makes families want to keep coming back for more. From the moment I stepped into the front office, Ms. Doris had me thinking, *This is a school that promotes a positive culture.* That's the power of a single person!

I've walked into hundreds of front offices across the country, and I've learned that you can tell a lot about a school's culture from those first few moments.

Take a moment to think about your own school.

Is there an expectation for how someone is greeted?

How do students and staff respond to visitors they meet in the hallways—as strangers or as welcomed guests?

"Each time I'd arrive in a new city, I'd get lost in the streets and photograph everything that looked interesting, taking nearly a thousand photographs every day. After each day of shooting, I'd select thirty or forty of my favorite photographs and post them on Facebook. I named the albums after my first impressions of each city."

BRANDON STANTON, AMERICAN PHOTOGRAPHER AND AUTHOR

NERVIOSO (ADAM)

Occasionally I am brought to schools to conduct professional development for parent groups. Once I was hired to conduct a session with a group of parents during a lunchtime event. I was told that a group of parents who were taking classes at the local community college would be attending. That's all the information I had.

I showed up and saw eleven women sitting in the media center chatting up and laughing with one another. When I walked into the room, the instructor for the course looked at me and said, "Do you speak Spanish?"

My eyebrows shot up. "Do they speak English?"

They did, sort of. The women were learning English. They were, for the most part, beginners, and my Spanish *es no bueno*. Thankfully, we were able to find a translator to help me out. As I got to the part in my presentation where I talk about impressions and walking into a school, I broke away from my typical presentation because I had a genuine question. Through the translator, I asked: "How do you feel when you walk into your child's school?"

All at once, and as if I had held up a cue card with the answer, they answered in unison, "*Nervioso.*" There was no translation needed for that emotion.

Several of the women spoke about how scary it was walking into the school, especially when not one person in the office could translate for them. One woman told me she did not finish elementary school in her home country, so she felt dumb when she walked into the school. Can you imagine walking into an unfamiliar place where you did not speak the language, feeling ill-equipped, and suddenly you are expected to advocate on behalf of your child?

Ensuring that *all* parents and community members feel welcomed and supported in our schools is part of what defines the limitless school. Language, socioeconomic status, and educational background should not determine the impression guests feel when they enter what may be an unfamiliar or scary place.

TIP *To ensure that guests feel welcomed in the school, schools can create a uniform and unified message or welcome that is verbalized to visitors. For example, when answering the phone, a consistent message can be, "Good morning/afternoon, thank you for calling [school name]. This is [person's name]; how can we help you today?" Even this small routine greatly impacts an outsider's first impression of your school.*

THE AJ WAY

Allen Jay Prep has eleven All-Star Expectations that every scholar knows and practices. One of those eleven is to greet visitors with a handshake and welcome them to the school. This is an expectation at Allen Jay, not an option. When scholars come to the school as fifth graders, the staff models for scholars the correct way to shake hands and greet people with a smile, and they work with the student to come up with appropriate questions to ask visitors so that conversations won't go stale.

It takes time to teach and model these expectations, but being able to walk down a hallway with a visitor, knowing that students will greet him or her and ask to show them around, gives our staff confidence in the impression Allen Jay makes with visitors. Our guests feel a sense of belonging that leaves a lasting impression. After all, no one wants to feel like they're a burden when they visit a school.

Every community member, parent, board member, superintendent, or other visitor who comes through Allen Jay always has many positive things to say when they leave the school. The best remark to hear is that the scholars were warm, inviting, and impressive. This is a testament to the expectation level of greeting visitors and adults who enter the building, no matter the time of day or occasion.

S.P.E.C.I.A.L.

Reading about what Allen Jay and other schools have done to make good impressions and create a positive culture may be inspiring, but you might be left with questions about how to make those things happen in your own school. First, let's understand what we're talking about. The idea of introducing yourself to a stranger or a guest and having them think highly about your school comes down to making a positive first impression. If we accept the fact that making a strong first impression is a learned skill, much like learning factorization, complex text structures, or the parts of the cell, then we can teach it as we would any of those academic standards.

Using practical experiences, research, and implementation opportunities, Adam created a system called S.P.E.C.I.A.L. that breaks down how to make a positive impression when encountering someone.

Shake Hands: Not too hard, not too soft. With enough practice and feedback, you'll master the art of an appropriately firm handshake.

Posture: Standing up straight exudes confidence. Given that other people are always reading our body language, confidence can go a long way in making a positive impression.

Eye Contact: Maintaining eye contact with the person you're meeting tells them you are interested in hearing what they have to say.

Charm: Offering a warm smile, nodding your head in agreement, or laughing at something funny shows charm, which makes you more likable and memorable.

Introduce Yourself: A great way to start an interaction with someone new is by saying your name. It serves as an excellent icebreaker.

Ask a Question: After you say your name, it's customary to ask the other person a question. Even a simple "How are you?" goes a long way in making a positive first impression.

Lean in and Listen: As you begin asking a question, make a slight lean in to show you're interested in what they are saying and be sure to listen so that you may respond with another question. We call this a conversation!

Making a S.P.E.C.I.A.L. first impression is a skill set that must be continually practiced. Remember, practice makes permanent. It must also be made clear to students that this is a starting guide. We are humans, and no two interactions will ever be the same. It becomes important to let students have opportunities experiencing various situations and scenarios so that they become more flexible and quick-thinking in their first impressions. Below are ways in which you and your school can build a positive school culture around making positive impressions:

- Teachers, stand in front of your door so that students have to stop and shake your hand and give a warm greeting before entering the classroom.

- Create a classroom job where a certain student(s) is the classroom greeter. Anytime a guest walks into the room (principal, parent, another teacher), that student is to quietly get out of their seat and greet them. Depending on who the guest is, the student should either head back to their seat, have a brief conversation with the guest, or invite them to observe the class learning.

- Administrators, stay in the hallways during transitions and set a goal to interact with at least ten students by shaking hands and greeting each other during class changes.

- Parents, have your child introduce themselves to your friends, colleagues, or new people you meet when you're in public together.

- Community members and board members, be deliberate when at a school or out in the community to provide opportunities for students to practice making introductions. Be a model and demonstrate positive interactions with fellow adults and students.

- All adults, don't take for granted that your skills are forever set in stone. Continually seek to improve your handshake, conversational skills, and charm. Have a professional development night at your school to give adults opportunities to refine their skills and network.

The keys to making these practices stick are providing constant opportunities and immediate feedback. When a student has her eyes on the ground as she greets you, stop her and have her do it again. If a student's handshake was like a floppy fish, have him try it again with a firmer grip. It does no good to ignore poor execution of a skill or to offer feedback hours later; feedback needs to be specific and immediate.

While I (Adam) was conducting a day of professional development at a middle school on the West Coast, the principal asked me about finding ways to enhance the school culture and bringing in "soft skills" so that students could interact more positively with one another. In between class transitions, I stood with the principal outside in the courtyard (which, by the way, is a fantastic perk of living in a place that is usually warm).

The principal and I must have put on Harry Potter's invisibility cloak because we seemed to be non-existent to the students passing by. They walked right past us without as much as even a grunt of acknowledgment. The

> "My belief is you have one chance to make a first impression."
>
> KEVIN McCARTHY,
> AMERICAN CONGRESSMAN

principal, recognizing the trend, began intentionally greeting students, but they continued to walk by without a word. Eventually, I told him that the only way student behavior would change is if he stopped students and made them aware that they needed to respond when someone greets them.

At the end of the day, I met with the entire staff in the media center where the principal relayed what happened in the courtyard. Acting on what I had said, he told his staff that he had spent the rest of the day being intentional about stopping students and making them "try again" when they did not acknowledge him when he said hi. He said that each student he did this to didn't mind changing their behavior; it had simply never been an expectation before. He admitted that it was an eye-opener for him and a good opportunity to see that students will rise to our expectations.

When all stakeholders recognize that creating a positive impression impacts school culture—and that change happens when expectations are raised—the school culture begins bleeding into the community culture. Students interact with adults differently as they eat in restaurants, go to performances, or shop in retail stores. Ultimately, these skills translate into more prepared and qualified individuals to interview for college and careers.

TURKEYS AND HANDSHAKES (ABE)

Shortly before Thanksgiving, the Allen Jay Prep MOD Squad made plans to reach out to the school community to help serve those in need. The boys planned to raise money through small fundraising efforts, and with every dollar matched by the PTA, the boys were going to go to Walmart to purchase turkeys for less fortunate families for Thanksgiving.

The fundraising efforts were a success, and the boys gathered the money to go to the local Walmart to buy turkeys. Keeping soft skills in mind, we always remind our scholars to use their manners and be on their best behavior when we leave the school campus, regardless of where we are going.

We entered Walmart and were greeted instantly. One of our MOD Squad boys, Taj, took the opportunity to extend his hand to the greeter, which caught her off-guard. He shook her hand and asked how her day was going, and she politely answered. As we made our way back to the frozen-food section of the store, the boys were smiling and making eye contact with other shoppers in hopes of making their day a little better.

After loading up the entire cart with turkeys, the boys made their way to the checkout line where another MOD squad member, Joe, struck up a conversation with the cashier. He told her all about the mission of buying the turkeys and how excited they were to pass out the turkeys to the families in need of a little boost during the holiday season. The cashier was impressed by the giving spirit of the boys, but she was more impressed by the boys' interpersonal skills.

On the way out the door, a sharply dressed gentleman wearing a Walmart badge stopped us. He introduced himself as the general manager of that Walmart and asked if we had a few minutes to chat. He told them that he watched them go around the store and the spirit and soft skills they possessed were unmatched, especially for their age. He asked us if we would like to join him in the conference area for lunch and to tell him more about their school and why the boys were buying so many turkeys. Of course, we jumped at the opportunity with excitement!

Once we were in the conference room, not only did the boys get invaluable practice using their soft skills while eating with a general manager of Walmart, but they were also able to answer questions and practice how to carry on conversations while eating. This lunch alone would have been rewarding enough for the boys. The manager was so impressed with the service project and the way the boys represented themselves and the school, he decided that he wanted to be a part of the giving in some way. He told us that he would be right back. We all wondered aloud what he was doing; some of the boys thought he was going to bless us all with a card that gave us unlimited supplies and access to Walmart. I told them I don't know if something like that even existed and to not get their hopes up! Instead, the manager came back in with a giant check, the kind you see on Publishers Clearing House commercials, and presented the MOD Squad boys and the school with $1,000. We were blown away! All of the boys shook his hand and told him how grateful they were to receive such a great donation.

The boys did something that day that, to them, felt normal. Good manners are an expectation for them; it's what they know. But to outsiders, simple courtesies delivered by middle schoolers came as a surprise. These boys made an excellent first impression. From the moment they walked into the store, they greeted people with a firm handshake and a smile. Their posture and eye contact showed confidence as did their ability to carry on conversations with different people. The soft skills that they had practiced daily at school led them to a great opportunity.

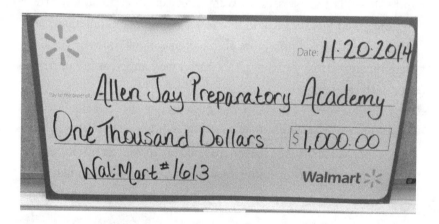

Not every handshake, smile, conversation, or charm will lead your students to a check from Walmart. However, the long-lasting effects of teaching students soft skills will instill valuable life lessons about proper social interactions, which no check could ever buy.

AMAZING SHAKE (ADAM)

In my first year working at the Ron Clark Academy, Ron came up with a contest to challenge the students to put their soft skills to the test. We called it the Amazing Shake, and it involved each student going around to various "stations," testing their quick-thinking capabilities and social awareness in a variety of situations. For instance, my station was simple: come introduce yourself to me. However, my right arm (which we are accustomed to shaking hands with) was tucked inside my shirt, so students had to figure out what to do. Do you shake with your left hand? Do you do a right hand/left hand shake? Do you skip the handshake all together? Students had to think quickly and decisively in order to make a good first impression on me, even if they weren't sure what to do.

This contest has continued through the years at Ron Clark Academy and now challenges students to conquer even more intense opportunities like "working a room" with executive board members for Delta Airlines, making a speech on the steps of the Georgia Capitol Building with angry protesters shouting at you, and interviewing with Barbara Corcoran from *Shark Tank*. While those tasks may not be a reality for every school, that has not stopped teachers and schools across the country from implementing their own version of an Amazing Shake.

A high school English teacher from Maryville, Tennessee, named Penny Ferguson has implemented her own version of the contest in her classroom. This veteran teacher of almost forty years never stops seeking new ideas to try with her students, and when she decided to try this contest with her students, she sought out community members to help her make it happen. After year one, word spread about the success of it, and she got funding from her principal to make it even bigger, including the opportunity to take the finalists to Nashville overnight!

In northwest Illinois, School District 205 created the Great Galesburg Shake, which was initiated by a small group of teachers who had visited the Ron Clark Academy and was eventually latched onto by the entire district and community. The contest has grown to tremendous heights over the years and now includes trips to Chicago for the finalists and more than thirty community sponsors and donors. If you Google the "Great Galesburg Shake," you'll see articles and resources that they have shared for how they have made this contest a community bonding experience and a celebration of the wonderful students that they have in their district.

Your smile, your handshake,
your listening ear can be the
difference maker in another
person's day.
Never underestimate the power
of *you*.

ABE & ADAM

3

MARRIAGE

(ABE)

I n the spring of 2013, I took a field trip with my school to a local base-ball game. My students were having a blast, and, during the seventh-inning stretch, my group decided it was time for yet another ice cream run. While standing in line with my students, I caught a glimpse of a teacher from another school. I had never seen her before and was intrigued by her. (This is a professional way of saying that I was attracted to her.) It wasn't one of those "lock-eyes" moments. It was *more*. It felt as if I were looking at someone whom I had known forever, but I had no idea who she was. Then, in a flash, one of my students yanked me back to reality by tugging on my arm and asking me a question about what to order. When I looked back toward where the goddess teacher had stood, she was gone. What could I do but go back to helping my twelve students order ice cream?

That evening, I received a phone call from Kevin Wheat, principal of the newly announced and innovative middle school, Allen Jay Prep. Dr. Wheat had watched me teach a lesson a few weeks prior to the field trip in anticipation of potentially hiring me as one of the first four teachers to start Allen Jay. On that call, he offered me the job and told me about an upcoming enrollment night that would give our future students an opportunity to meet the teachers.

At the enrollment night, I pulled up to the school parking lot filled with excitement about this new journey. I walked into the building and saw the other newly hired staff there handing out T-shirts and pizza. As I was grabbing a plate for pizza, another staff member, who was getting a bottle of water from a cooler, greeted me with a big smile and said, "Hi! I'm Brittany, and we are going to be teammates!"

> "Chains do not hold a marriage together. It is threads, hundreds of tiny threads, which sew people together through the years."
>
> SIMONE SIGNORET,
> FRENCH CINEMA ACTRESS

Fumbling over my words, because here in front of me was this goddess teacher, I sputtered out an unimpressive introduction. "Hi, Brittany, it's nice to meet you; I'm Abe." We spent the rest of the evening together hanging out and meeting the new kids who would be joining us in just a few months.

After a long evening, I got back into my car and headed home. A friend called me to see how everything went. She peppered me with questions about what the school was going to be about, what my classroom looked like, what theme I was going to use, and so on. And all I said to her was, "Weezie, I met my future wife tonight." I explained to her that my newly found teammate named Brittany was the same woman I had seen at the baseball game months before and had a special feeling about. After spending the evening around the school with her, I knew we were going to be something more than just teammates.

Long story short, Brittany and I were the first two teachers hired at Allen Jay Middle. Dr. Wheat had called Brittany and offered her a teaching position the same night he had called me. It was destiny; we had been brought together by this innovative school and a passion for education.

In the first year, Brittany taught fifth-grade math and science, and I taught fifth-grade language arts and social studies in the classroom next door. We had a blast. We planned great lessons together and really poured everything we had into the kids. Brittany and I shared a love for Chipotle and ate there together once a week, which turned into a few times a week, and then turned into hanging out every day after school. We officially began dating about two months into the school year.

In year two of Allen Jay, we moved into our newly built building and hired new staff members for the additional 100 scholars who would be entering our program. Brittany and I were on different teams that year, but our relationship remained strong, and our new teammates loved that there was a budding love story in the new Allen Jay building.

At the end of the year, I took Brittany to my old middle school in Charlotte, Piedmont Open Middle, which was a special place for me growing up. We walked out to the football field where a path of rose petals (laid out by her friends) led to a giant heart midfield. My parents were sitting on a bench with an iPad and had Brittany's mother on Facetime so she could see what was about to happen (Brittany's family lives in Indiana). I got down on one knee and asked this woman, who instantly intrigued me on that school field trip and whom I had grown to love as we taught together for the past two years, to marry me. She, thank goodness, said yes.

At the end of the school's third year, Brittany and I got married in Cleveland, North Carolina, in front of our friends and family. Dr. Wheat and other staff members sat in the front row, witnessing two people, whom they had come to know as colleagues and friends, dedicate the rest of their lives to each other.

While Adam and I wrote this book together, Brittany and I were waiting on our first child to arrive in July 2017. So if you are keeping score at home of the Brittany/Abe story:

Year One—Met and Dated

Year Two—Engaged

Year Three—Married

Year Four—Had a Baby

Year Five and Beyond—TBD

Adam and I decided to include this story in our book for a few reasons. First, the "M" stands for marriage, so it is apropos to start with a story about one! But more importantly, the values of marriage hold closely to the ideas that we believe help create a limitless school. As in marriage or any good relationship, the key components of communication, listening, compromise, and support help us build solid relationships in schools.

> "Wise men speak because they have something to say; fools because they have to say something."

PLATO, GREEK PHILOSOPHER

COMMUNICATION

In a good marriage or relationship, communication is essential. The same is true inside *and outside* your school.

If it isn't too painful, think about a relationship in your life that ended badly. What was the leading cause of its failure? Our guess is that the reason probably funnels down to poor communication by one or both parties. Miscommunication or *no* communication can lead to all sorts of misunderstandings, hurt feelings, and grievances. And when bad communication is habitual, those feelings sow the discord and discontent that ultimately ends in the death of a friendship, partnership, or marriage.

Now imagine a school that lacks communication. Maybe you are in a school like this now. How does this impact day-to-day operations? How do you turn it around? If you are part of a district or school that communicates very well, what do you do well? How can you get even better?

With Staff

We believe good communication starts with relaying the vision of the administrators. Administrators have a lot to juggle when it comes to communication. One simple and effective way to keep everyone on the same page is a weekly memo that outlines the upcoming week for your staff. These can be sent via email, social media, or by video, depending on what you're comfortable with. Weekly memos can state upcoming events, a vision for the week, and duties that need to be addressed. They are also a good place to highlight staff members' efforts and successes. Touching base weekly establishes clear and effective communication, which lends a hand in establishing positive culture.

With Parents

Administrators also need to communicate with parents. Above and beyond the weekly calls or emails you make to parents, it's important to connect with them at school functions. We have found that some of the most effective conversations with parents have been at sporting events. We use this time to talk to parents about positive things going on in their own lives or at school. It's helpful to keep the mood lighthearted and upbeat.

WITH COMMUNITY MEMBERS

When reaching out to community members to invite them to your school or to share their expertise with your students, be sure to make the mission of your school evident and clear. For instance, at Allen Jay, we regularly ask community members to speak at our school or to take our scholars on a tour related to their employment or passions. We have had a variety of guest speakers, including professional and college athletes, state leaders, business leaders, and parents. Invariably, one of the things we say to these individuals when we invite them to our school is, "At Allen Jay, we are a leadership-development school. We want our scholars to be on the pathway to college. Can you help us?"

Allen Jay reached out to a scholar's dad who happened to be a fraternity member. He came in and spoke with the scholars during a morning rally and did a step routine. He talked to the scholars about professional attire, interviews, and the pathway to college. As a parent and as a community member, having this young man's dad at our school was a positive culture-builder for students, teachers, and the school as a whole.

BE AWARE OF YOUR TONE

Finally, the tone of the communication is an important piece to consider for a successful marriage. As communication becomes more digital, voice inflection and intent get lost in a sea of characters on a screen. We must use our words carefully, especially as we discuss sensitive topics with others. When communicating digitally, remember that emotions and feelings can be misinterpreted. Being thoughtful, prompt, and professional are important to a fruitful relationship. As it stands, email remains a popular and convenient way to communicate among stake-holders, particularly between teachers and parents.

Let's put this idea of careful, thoughtfully chosen words to the test. Below is an example of two approaches toward communication between teacher and parent. As you read the two emails, consider the following:

Which do you think has a tone that the reader would appreciate more? Which mirrors your approach toward communicating with others?

EXAMPLE 1

Hi. Wanted to let you know DJ is failing my class. I have tried over and over in class to get him to calm down, and he won't stop talking. I need you to come in and meet with me and some of his other teachers that are having problems. This Friday at 11:00 a.m. would work best. Thanks.

EXAMPLE 2

Good Evening,

I hope you're doing well. I wanted to reach out to share a couple observations I have noticed with DJ. He hasn't performed to his fullest potential the past few weeks on quizzes, and he is missing a few homework assignments, which is unlike him.

DJ has also struggled keeping his focus in class. I have moved his seat and asked him if there is anything I can do to help him, but he continues to distract himself and others. I wanted to reach out because we both want DJ to be successful, and I would like us to brainstorm ways together that he can find success in my class and work to his fullest potential.

Would you mind coming in or talking over the phone about possible strategies that we can put together to help DJ moving forward? Please let me know times that may work for you.

Thank you and I hope to hear from you soon.

The goal of these emails is the same: improving the child's behavior and focus in class. But the tone of the first email feels harsh and confrontational. The second comes across as an invitation to the parent to partner with the teacher for the child's benefit. If you were the parent in this situation, which would you want to receive?

Clear, concise, and transparent communication goes a long way toward building and maintaining a fruitful marriage within any school's culture. Strong communication can ease stress levels and prevent conflicts by eliminating misunderstandings. By sharing openly and clearly, you can build a culture that ensures that all stakeholders feel free to speak their mind. And that's when you can communicate your respect for others by listening.

LISTENING

We have two ears and one mouth for a reason: to listen more than we speak. In the world of education, speaking is a lot more common than listening. School is one of those entities about which everyone has an opinion and at least some personal experience—if not as an educator, then as a student or parent. It's not that offering those opinions is bad, but if we want our ideas to be well received, we must understand that there are times it's appropriate to speak up and times when listening is our best course of action. Just like in any good relationship, listening is a key ingredient for success. Let's face it, people like to be heard!

At most board of education meetings, there is an open forum time during which any community member can approach the microphone and share a concern or thought. Board members hear varying viewpoints on a wide range of topics, from zoning and testing to controversial topics like transgender bathrooms and immigration. It is unlikely that everyone in the room will agree upon every topic, and that's okay as long as every person has the opportunity to be heard—even if their view is unpopular. When you learn to listen first and speak second, you can engage in more civil, respectful debate and make positive change.

An Orange County, Florida, board of education member named Rick Roach had listened to the concerns from educators, students, and parents about the state's standardized tests. In response to those concerns, he took his district's tenth-grade standardized test. He failed. He explained in a now viral interview that the results indicated that he was a poor reader, even though this is a man who has multiple degrees and is an elected member of the school district. As a result of his experience, he became more vocal about testing reform and questioning the process in which we evaluate "success" in students. He pondered how he would have thought about himself if he had taken this test as a tenth grader, and he had a better understanding of how students judge themselves harshly based on test scores. This board member began his inquiry into the testing culture simply by listening. He could have easily dismissed the concerns as complaints, but instead he decided to be an upstander and become more informed on the issue.

> "To listen well is as powerful a means of communication and influence as to talk well."
>
> JOHN MARSHALL, AMERICAN POLITICIAN AND CHIEF JUSTICE

COMPROMISE

The Rolling Stones sang a song titled, "You Can't Always Get What You Want." That message loudly echoes in marriages and relationships, and it rings true for school stakeholders as well. As we just mentioned above, it is unrealistic to think we can get every person in our school communities to agree on every topic. Then how do we find middle ground?

Compromise is the art of giving a little to get a little. It's an act that allows for diverse viewpoints to be heard and gives people peace of mind—both of which are important if you want your culture cube to be aligned!

As an administrator, you are hit hard each day with the need to make tough decisions. Let's say you are a principal and have a teacher who is looking to redecorate her room. She wants to paint the walls in bright colors, which the district has a strict policy against. You don't want to completely turn it down because you know it's a good idea and will enhance the school and classroom culture. You meet with her and explain that the district has a tough policy against this, but there is nothing against painting the wooden cabinets or the tiled ceilings in the classroom. Obviously, it may not have been exactly what the teacher wanted to hear, but instead of simply saying no and destroying a good idea, you found a way to compromise in this situation and still make this teacher feel empowered to improve her classroom.

Compromise doesn't mean you need to settle. Continue to fight for what you believe in, but be sure to put yourself in the other person's shoes. Through compromise, you can strengthen the culture of trust and set a precedent for how you deal with conflict. In our experiences, schools with a positive culture often have leaders who are skilled in compromise. That doesn't mean those leaders have a reputation for being "soft." Rather, their staff and community have come to trust them to handle conflict in a way that reveals a high degree of thoughtfulness and respect.

"Compromise works well in this world when you have shared goals."

JIM DEMINT, AMERICAN WRITER
AND POLITICIAN

SUPPORT

You would be hard pressed to find a marriage that doesn't go through tough times at some point. Maybe a spouse lost a job, there was a death in the family, or the kids were driving you up a wall. It's in the trying and stressful times that you rely on your spouse for support. That's what strong marriages are about: knowing that you have a shoulder to cry on or a person who will listen without judgment. In schools, having a system that allows individuals to be supported in times of need is important to the maintenance of a positive culture. The reality is that we are all human, and emotions can drive our decisions and our ability to perform, which is why it's unrealistic to think that a student who just saw her mother sent to jail should be expected to excel on a state exam the next morning or that a teacher who stayed up all night with her sick child will teach her best lesson during a formal observation the next day.

Support can come in many different forms. Both of us have been in meetings with parents who entered the room angry, but before the meeting ended, they had calmed down and found ways to work with the teacher or administration. In most cases, all these parents really needed was to vent; their frustrations really weren't aimed at us. Listening, in circumstances like this, provides a valuable form of support and gives you the opportunity to understand and clear up any miscommunication.

We have also both had students who needed a more tangible form of support: a new jacket, book bag, or school supplies. In those instances, we have reached out to our school's community to help with small purchases to help support that student. It's one thing to hear about a need, but support means taking action.

And finally, we have both worked with colleagues who needed support with anything from helping to plan a lesson to hitching a ride to pick up a car at the auto repair shop. Simple acts, like taking time to brainstorm or to share your time (or commute) with a coworker, can build connection and culture.

There are a number of small ways to support people that make a big impact. Leave a note on a child's desk that says, "I believe in you!" If you're a principal, drop a note in a teacher's mailbox with the words, "Thanks for all you do! Let me know how I can help." Those simple gestures go a long way. In our busy lives and fast-paced world, it's easy to forget to support the ones we love the most. Any healthy relationship requires small acts of kindness; whether it's leaving a note or offering a few encouraging words, stakeholders need to be reminded that we are here for each other.

When I (Adam) was a fifth-grade teacher at Endhaven Elementary in Charlotte, I was fortunate to work with a fantastic staff. They were there for the right reasons and worked incredibly hard each day. I decided one year to create a 5k race in our local school neighborhood to help raise money for Levine Children's Hospital. I called it the Kids4Kids5k, and I was stoked to have hundreds of people run for a great cause. But then I realized that planning the event was threatening to engulf my life. I couldn't believe how much work goes into planning these events. Just as I was starting to drown in this venture, I was thrown a lifeline by my two colleagues, Terrance and Kelly. Terrance began organizing the volunteers for the event, and Kelly took on the sponsorship responsibilities. Together, the three of us organized a successful fundraiser and event for the community. Their support came just at the right time and in just the right way, and because of it, we were able to provide a great bonding moment for the school and community.

Supporting those around you, especially when you yourself need support, can seem daunting. You may even wonder, *How am I supposed to help another person when it feels like I'm drowning in my own life?* Our best answer is that life has a funny way of helping out those who help others. Just when you think no one is there for you, look to help someone else who is in need and watch how support can come full circle back to you.

SCENARIOS

Empathy is another essential skill in marriage; putting yourself in the other person's metaphorical shoes helps you understand how that person may feel. One of the better ways to accomplish this is through role play. When we conduct Limitless School workshops with groups, we often have audience members join us on stage to participate in role play. The goal is to allow people to practice and reflect upon how to react in various situations.

We typically give each participant a description of an event told from a particular point of view. After they read the scenario, they sit down for a mock meeting to discuss the situation and look to find a solution. For example, here is a scenario of a parent meeting with a principal about a student who has been absent a great deal.

Jacob's principal: Your attendance secretary has informed you that sixteen-year-old Jacob has been absent thirteen of the past fourteen days. None of the absences are excused, and his teachers have not heard from him. One teacher mentioned that she heard a rumor that he's been on the streets during the day. Obviously, if Jacob's not in school, he can't learn the material, and you would like to figure out how you can get Jacob the help he needs to be successful and graduate. You'll be meeting with Jacob's dad to discuss this.

Jacob's dad: Your son Jacob is sixteen years old and has been absent for thirteen of the past fourteen days of school. The family has been struggling financially, and every person needs to pull their weight to help keep food on the table and the lights on, and this includes Jacob. You found Jacob a job at the local corner store, and the only shift they had available was during school hours. This shouldn't last much longer as they expect to have a second-shift spot opening up, but in the meantime, earning money for the family is the most important thing. Jacob's school has called to have a meeting since they are concerned that he has not been in school. You expected this phone call, but they need to understand the circumstance.

After a role play interaction like this, we usually debrief with the participants to discuss how they felt in that role. We ask them to identify key points that the other person said that affected them one way or another. We also open up discussion to the audience to garner feedback and ideas. This type of activity is valuable in a classroom setting, administrative training, parent workshops, and beyond. It opens conversation and allows participants to be introspective into how another person may see a situation.

A healthy marriage requires each individual to commit to communicating, listening, compromising, and supporting because when times get tough, those skills will be what helps the marriage survive and thrive. Schools with a positive culture embody these four attributes. When problems arise, stakeholders have the know-how to sit down with one another and work through the issues side by side. They understand that there are many marriages within the school, and each one has value and importance toward being limitless.

We always say that we marry
"our best friend." If the values
of marriage are going to be
what drives our culture at
school, we are going to have
a lot of best friends!

ABE & ADAM

4

INTEGRITY

f someone told you that you could live a financially and socially comfortable life with a job that you loved, there's a good chance you'd jump at the opportunity. In all respects, Tim Donaghy had just that. Not only did Donaghy marry the love of his life, he was working in his dream job as a basketball referee. He had spent five years working his way up the ranks as a high school referee when he was approached by the Continental Basketball Association (CBA). After working hard in the CBA and staying by the book, he was offered a referee position in the National Basketball Association (NBA), the highest level of professional basketball. The average salary of an NBA official is six figures! Not a bad gig for Mr. Donaghy!

All his career, Tim Donaghy was known as a referee who played by the rules and called the game fairly. Then, one day during his time with the NBA, a friend asked him about potentially altering a game so that the outcome would benefit his friend's gambling. Donaghy scoffed at the idea at first until he realized what the betting line was. That night, Tim Donaghy made a decision that forever altered his life.

After a couple of seasons of betting on games and making calls that altered game outcomes, Donaghy was turned in by an informant to the FBI and charged with a federal crime. Here was a guy who had it all: good money, a respected job, and a loving family. Yet he traveled down a dangerous path that ultimately landed him in prison.

Frankly put, Tim Donaghy lost his integrity. Integrity defines who we are and what we stand for; it's a character trait we want for ourselves and our students. It can be hard, however, to live a life of integrity, and it's even harder to teach this vital life skill, which is why all stakeholders must intentionally work to bring integrity to the forefront as a defining feature of our schools' cultures.

We believe in three concrete ways that integrity can be brought into your school's culture: verbiage, actions, and reflection. Through these three practices, stakeholders can more easily wrap their minds around how to define and instill a sense of integrity across the school.

> "The greatness of a man is not in how much wealth he acquires, but in his integrity and his ability to affect those around him positively."
>
> BOB MARLEY, JAMAICAN SINGER AND SONGWRITER

VERBIAGE

Our words matter. Whether someone hears them or not, we build our character around what we say. When a teacher sits around the lunch table with colleagues and says how much she hates her class, but then tells the kids she loves them when she's with them, she's not demonstrating strong integrity. Her character is damaged by the hateful words she expresses when she thinks others aren't listening. When an assistant principal sits around a table with teachers during a grade-level meeting and says that a teacher from another grade level needs to be fired, that puts a diminishing mark on the assistant principal's character. Her teachers then wonder what she says about them when they are not around.

We're all prone to negative speak (e.g., complaining or gossiping). It's human nature. We find comfort in complaining about things we don't agree with or people who annoy us. The true test of character is how we stand against or give into this knee-jerk response.

At a middle school that was struggling with the way its faculty and staff were talking about parents and students, a group of teachers decided a change needed to occur. Tired of hearing nothing but negative talk, these teacher-leaders approached the school improvement team and offered a solution. They recognized that the majority of the negative talk occurred during lunchtime when the teachers were in the teachers' lounge. Rather than condemn or call out the negative behavior, the team put a conversation starter menu on the teachers' lounge table and asked teachers to use these suggestions when they started conversations about their day.

Positive sentence stems like, "I was really proud of ____ this morning when he/she ____" or "I had a light-bulb moment from ____ this morning when he/she ____," replaced phrases like "I hate it when ____ does ____" and "They annoyed me so much this morning."

If our words become our character, then finding the brightest moments to highlight in our conversations illuminates us in a positive way. And when one person speaks positively, it often inspires others to follow suit.

There are also many ways for stakeholders to use positive speak to build school culture. During board of education meetings, members can take the time to recognize at least three employees in the district for exemplary work by reading a story about the incredible things they do. Principals can share stories at staff meetings about teachers who have gone above and beyond to help others in the school. Teachers can make phone calls home explaining how their child did an exceptional job at school. Parents can ask their child how their teacher taught them something new today.

Again, our words matter. People internalize the good and bad that are said about them. If we are to make a school culture that values and embraces positive speak, then we need to be intentional about finding positive words to describe all stakeholders.

What I Didn't Say (Abe)

Sometimes it's what we don't say that really matters. I learned this the hard way one day when I was scheduled to be the administrative representative for an Individualized Education Plan (IEP) meeting for a student. My principal was out of the building, and it

"The strength of a nation derives from the integrity of the home."

CONFUCIUS, CHINESE TEACHER AND PHILOSOPHER

was simply a hectic day. I almost forgot about this meeting, rushed in just as it was starting, and gave a quick smile to the parent. The meeting went smoothly, and I left before the official end of the meeting because I had other issues to tend to around the building.

About an hour later, this parent called the school and asked to speak to the principal. In a nutshell, the parent was insulted that I hadn't said anything to her during the meeting. The principal covered for me and apologized to the mother, which smoothed over the situation. This incident shows an important point, though. Sometimes what we don't say can be just as harmful as what we do say. The parent felt slighted by my silence, especially since our school took pride in our relationships with our school community. My character, in this parent's eyes, had been tainted.

Looking back, I certainly could have given this mother a "hello" and "how are you" when I walked in, versus just a smile. It was nothing against her; I was simply going through the motions of the meeting, overwhelmed by all the things going on that day. That's certainly not an excuse, though. And it isn't in alignment with the inviting, family-like atmosphere we strive for at Allen Jay. For this mother, that IEP meeting may have been the most important or emotional part of her day, and my lack of words were bothersome to her—which matters.

Again, our words matter, and in this case, a lack of words matter. As stakeholders in this marriage, as we discussed before, communication is essential as we build individual and school integrity. We must be as alert to when we don't speak as to when we do. And as I learned from this moment, hearing warm and welcoming words can impact how people view our school.

ACTIONS

The true test of character is what we do when no one is looking. How we hold ourselves in public frequently labels us, but how we conduct ourselves in private ultimately defines us. For instance, the sixth-grade student who is kind, polite, and giving while in the presence of teachers, but sends four-letter-word-laced texts to friends to describe their school, is exhibiting polarizing integrity. The student is labeled as a "sweet kid" by the teachers at school, but internally he knows he's just putting on a show when in public.

One of the things that makes it difficult to measure true integrity is the fact that we aren't usually privy to another person's private life. To remedy this, it becomes important for us to "catch" people in moments when they don't think someone is watching to understand their true integrity. Did you see a student picking up trash off the ground because it was the right thing to do? Did you catch a community member buying a student dinner because they knew that they were short on money? Did you hear about a teacher who brought a student's work to their house because they've been sick?

With the prevalence of camera phones and videos of people being caught "doing the right thing" popping up online, these acts still seem surprising. Much like the "upstander" mentioned in the Leadership chapter, those who consciously make decisions to help others or turn away from bad choices have a high sense of integrity. It is encouraging to see these videos being shared and talked about because they provide a model for others to emulate. Our students are impressionable, and seeing actions of high integrity being celebrated leaves a mark on their minds that these are behaviors to embrace.

THE TEACHERLESS CLASS (ADAM)

It's early February and a third-grade class calmly walks down the hallway in an urban elementary school in Texas. They are returning from their art class, which is located on an adjacent hall from their classroom. This in itself may not be anything shocking. What you may be surprised to hear is that their teacher, Ms. Bonner, is nowhere to be found. She is waiting outside the classroom for the class to return safely and quietly. And they do. Just as they've done each day for the past several weeks.

Like little soldiers, the twenty-two students return to their class with smiles on their faces as they pass by Ms. Bonner and get prepared for reading workshop. This privilege did not come overnight. It took months for Ms. Bonner to instill a sense of integrity in her students through maintaining high expectations, providing opportunities and feedback, and building relationships. Over time, she was able to release responsibility to the students to take on this simple, yet meaningful, freedom to return to the classroom on their own.

I was able to witness this class in person while at the school. As impressed as I was with this demonstration, I was disappointed that, from what I learned, Ms. Bonner's class was the only group in the school that did this. How was it possible that only twenty-two students in the entire school could handle this responsibility? What was lacking in the other classrooms that the other teachers didn't have the confidence to allow their students the same opportunity?

Integrity is bottled up inside many of our students, waiting to be tested. It's up to us as adults to provide opportunities for our students to demonstrate it. Ms. Bonner could just as easily have been teaching another grade or at another school and likely would have been able to have her students do the same thing. But when other teachers or stakeholders look at Ms. Bonner's class and think, *Well if I had those kids, I could do that too*, they are missing the point; their kids may well have the same potential—it just hasn't been tapped yet. Rather than being discouraged by others' results, recognize that one person's success can be a stepping stone for all. Raise your expectations, let trust grow, and open opportunities to test and strengthen your students' integrity. As you do so, integrity gets etched into the culture of the school.

SOCCER COACH (ADAM)

My younger brother Marc has been a sports fanatic from the time we were young. He was the kid who would memorize statistics and team schedules. A fun afternoon for him was watching game tapes and drawing up new plays. He turned that obsession into coaching, and for the past two decades, has been coaching various sports at different levels.

He had been the boys' junior varsity soccer coach at a high school for a number of years with massive success. The girls' varsity soccer coach position at the school opened up one summer, and he was interested in applying for it. The new athletic director narrowed the search down to two people: Marc, and a woman who had been the girls' junior varsity coach the year before. The woman was young and had only that one year of coaching experience behind her. In the end, because she was a teacher in the district, Marc was told that she was going to be given the job.

Like most districts, all hires need to be approved by the board of education after recommendations by the school. When it came time for the woman to be approved for the girls' varsity coaching job, one of the board members—who had a son Marc had coached a few years prior and closely followed the soccer programs in the town—was befuddled as to why they hired the woman over Marc. When the board member discovered that the reason came down to being in-house versus merit and experience, he talked with the other board members, and they took the vote off the table that night. He told the superintendent that there were questions about the hiring process and they would need to re-interview for the position and do a more thorough job examining candidate qualifications. Marc ended up getting the job and, in his first six years with the girls' program, has brought home a state sectional title and the school's first-ever conference title for girls' soccer.

The point of this story is not about sports or coaching. The focus, for us, is on the board of education member, who had the integrity to fight for what he believed was right. It would have been easy as a board member to want to get through an agenda without controversy so they could finish up the night. In reality, a soccer coaching position was not the most pressing issue at the school, so for this board member to go out on a limb for Marc and call into question ethical hiring practices, showed a lot about his character. By doing what he did, he established a culture that hiring needs to be about qualifications and merit, not just the quick fix.

> "Real integrity is doing the right thing, knowing that nobody's going to know whether you did it or not."
>
> OPRAH WINFREY, AMERICAN MEDIA PROPRIETOR

To demonstrate the shift in practice that has resulted, Marc has subsequently interviewed a couple of times for social studies teaching positions at this high school, and he has been passed up in favor of people who have higher degrees or better qualifications. While it's certainly not pleasant being told you got beat out, he understands and respects the reasons.

REFLECTION (ABE)

At Allen Jay, the entire school assembles each morning in the gym for something we call rally. Rally is a combination of student-led announcements, high-energy celebrations, motivational messages, and character-building lessons led by Dr. Wheat or myself. You will find students rapping the lunch menu, competing in Minute-to-Win-It-type challenges, and dancing to the latest viral videos. It's a fun way to motivate scholars and staff each and every morning to get excited about school. Character building is one of the pillars that Allen Jay stands on, and morning rally gives scholars the opportunity to learn about and see examples of character in a variety of ways.

One week, we decided to highlight individuals who had struggled in life. During the morning rallies, we featured famous actors and athletes, people whom scholars would immediately recognize. One morning stands out in my memory more than others. We focused our character lesson on Tiger Woods. The narrative that we provided was that he had amassed an incredible amount of money through his golfing career, had won countless tournaments and prestigious awards, and had a fantastic family. These things came crashing down when people discovered that he had been living a secret, deceitful life. As Dr. Wheat told the story, I looked out into the audience and saw the scholars hooked on his words. The rally ended with an explanation that integrity doesn't have any best friends or favorites; it's about choosing to do the right things on your own when no one is looking. In my mind, I thought we hit a home run that morning!

When planning morning rallies or preparing presentations for kids, we are always conscious of the content we place in front of scholars. As Dr. Wheat and I reflected on that day's rally, we realized our message was flawed. By emphasizing the negative moments and mistakes of Tiger Woods without any sign of hope for recovery, we realized we may have conveyed a message that people can't bounce back from mistakes—once you're down and out, that's it. Clearly, that was not our intent, and reflecting on the rally allowed us to correct that potential confusion with our students the next day, demonstrate the integrity that we are looking to instill, and make it better next time.

It's never satisfying to realize that you've made an error in judgment, but to bring integrity into our schools, we must model it by remaining humble and fixing our mistakes. Reflective integrity requires a high level of awareness on your impact on those you touch and influence.

CLASS REPRESENTATIVE ELECTION (ADAM)

It was early in the school year, and we needed to elect class representatives for the student council. In the grand scheme of the craziness of teaching, this was barely on my radar. And although it wasn't much of a matter for me, I knew it was important to my fifth graders, so I wanted to make this a meaningful activity.

I asked my students to anonymously nominate classmates for the ballot and then allowed the nominated students to accept or reject the nomination. I ended up with three students on the ballot. On the list was Tommy, the most popular boy in the class. He had personality, he was handsome, and he liked being the center of attention. The problem was that he was lazy and an Eddie Haskell sort of kid. He would smile and be charming when you were looking, but the second you turned your back, he'd be up something. Next on the ballot was Lita. She was smart, kind, and responsible. She enjoyed helping others and got along with everyone. She remains one of the most genuine students I have ever taught. The third student was Brandon. He was a great kid and got along well with people, but he was not particularly made for this role.

It was no secret that many students were looking to vote for Tommy. The boys wanted to be like him, and the girls were in love with him, and, in fifth grade, those are the things that get votes in an election. I thought it would be valuable for the students to discuss the qualities that should be considered when electing representatives, so we had a class meeting to talk about it. The students came up with the character traits that you would expect them to say: hard worker, honest, responsible, and so on. Basically, they described Lita all on their own. But I still thought it would be a stretch for her to win; Tommy just had too much influence in the room.

Would you believe that when we voted, Lita ended up getting almost every vote! I was so proud of the kids for voting for the candidate who matched what they were looking for in a representative. This class showed me their integrity by reflecting upon the traits they wanted to see in a representative and voting for a peer who demonstrated great character on a daily basis. My students were building their own limitless classroom that year. The lesson that hit home with me was that when we provide students opportunity to reflect and demonstrate integrity, they can do pretty amazing things!

Integrity constructs a school's culture, kind of like how we say a building's physical structure has integrity. It's interesting, then, that certain buildings can't stay standing after a storm.

ABE & ADAM

5

TIME

Principal Lisa Burkhead knew she wanted to restructure her school's culture. The school, Fertitta Middle School, was a three-star (out of five) school in Clark County, Nevada, the fifth-largest school district in the country. Lisa's middle school is diverse—in all respects of the word—and serves about 1,500 students. She knew that to make changes, she would need to be strategic. As a relatively new principal to the school, demanding wide-spread changes and policies would simply not work. Staff and parents would be angered, and students could rebel. Lisa decided that to successfully roll out her vision, she'd need *time*.

It's hard to accept that changes might not come overnight or even during a school year. There's inherent pressure from district and state officials to improve, especially when a school is struggling. While Lisa's school was not failing, she knew they could be better. For her to accept that change would take time, she understood that she would need to mark celebrations and victories along the way to keep morale high for stakeholders *and* herself.

So how did Lisa lay out her vision? She identified five stages in her plan that would ultimately lead to her school going from a three-star to a five-star school in under three years.

STAGE 1: FIND YOUR MOTIVATION AND SUPPORT

Lisa heard Ron Clark speak in 2012 and was inspired to make a change in her own school. She knew change required support, however, so she spoke to her direct supervisor and a board of education trustee representative to get their blessing as well as resources for her vision. They visited the Ron Clark Academy together and began discussing what her proposed initiatives could look like in the public school setting. By including the leadership team from the start, Lisa was able to tap into their expertise to further develop the plan.

STAGE 2: IDENTIFY YOUR LEADERS AND BUILD A PLAN

After securing the support of her supervisors, Lisa identified the teacher-leaders in her school—those individuals who had respect from peers and were already making an impact in their classrooms. Those leaders, along with Lisa, conducted a needs-assessment survey of the school, looking at what teachers wanted. Lisa sent them to Atlanta to be trained at the Ron Clark Academy. The team of eight returned with fresh ideas and inspiration and continued to meet throughout the summer and fall to debrief on their experiences at the training and develop a plan for implementation. The meetings were open to all staff members, and input and feedback from teachers who did not attend the training was solicited after each session.

STAGE 3: SPREAD THE ENERGY

When it came time to spread the excitement to the staff members and ignite the fire in any who weren't yet on board, I (Adam) was brought in to do a series of on-site professional developments. I conducted workshops, modeled lessons, and met with teachers to discuss instructional practices. Participating in these experiences built a sense of community and trust among the staff that spread to the students and parents. The school implemented common practices and expectations across the school, such as respectful interactions (e.g., saying, "Yes, sir" or "Yes, ma'am," holding the door for people, and saying, "Thank you"). These expectations were part of the "Fertitta 15," a set of consistent school-wide behavior guidelines. Soon, parents began noticing the school's behavior expectations were being translated into practices at home. As a result, parents felt more a part of the school, and it showed in their willingness to be present. In 2014–2015 (year two of the transformation), parents logged more than 500 volunteer hours on campus; in 2015–2016, they registered over 1,700 hours.

STAGE 4: DON'T BITE OFF MORE THAN YOU CAN CHEW

With the energy spreading through Fertitta Middle School, it would have been easy to put the pedal to the floor and speed ahead. But the leadership team knew that if they rushed the progress, some people would be left behind. Instead, the school's leadership chose to master pieces of the puzzle before

> "You don't have to swing hard to hit a home run. If you got the timing, it'll go."
>
> YOGI BERRA, AMERICAN BASEBALL PLAYER

taking on the next challenge. For example, Fertitta implemented a House System (á la *Harry Potter*), and students and staff became committed to the idea of having small societies within their school. As this cemented, leaders carried out celebrations of the houses, such as house assemblies, student house leaders' elections, house-colored lanyards for ID badges, cafeteria booths for each house, bathroom transformations inspired by each house, and house crests painted on the school. Each of these pieces was carefully planned and executed over the course of three years.

Stage 5: Commitment

Lisa made a promise that any staff member who wished to go to Atlanta to the Ron Clark Academy would have an opportunity. In addition, each time Adam came to Fertitta, any staff member who wanted to see him teach would be scheduled to watch him. This commitment for continuing professional development gave each teacher and staff member ownership in the process of shifting the culture at Fertitta. Ultimately, these positive experiences for the staff spread into seeing increased morale and involvement for faculty, students, and parents. For three consecutive years, the school saw a steady improvement in district surveys, which indicated satisfaction and support from stakeholders in regard to the school culture.

Fertitta's success was not just recognized by staff and parents but by outsiders as well. School district officials and other school leaders were intrigued when they visited the school as students held the door open for them and called them "ma'am" or "sir." Students recognized the changes as well. It became normal to be kind to one another and support classmates. Culture at Fertitta Middle School changed. It took time, but stakeholders bought in to the change because they were involved in the process.

We will revisit Lisa and her school in the Success chapter when we talk about how we know when building a positive culture is working.

Time has several contexts in our society. Therefore, the rest of this chapter looks at time from different angles: patience, strategy, and perseverance. We cannot change or turn back time, so we must focus on how we can use it most wisely.

THE "NOT HAPPY" EMAIL (ADAM)

I received an email from a parent (whom I really liked) one evening with the subject line reading "Not Happy." Suddenly I felt that sinking feeling in the pit of my stomach. A thousand thoughts ran through my head about what I could have done that caused a parent to be "not happy" with me.

"Never cut a tree down in the wintertime. Never make a negative decision in the low time. Never make your most important decisions when you are in your worst moods. Wait. Be patient. The storm will pass. The spring will come."

ROBERT H. SCHULLER, AMERICAN MOTIVATIONAL SPEAKER AND AUTHOR

Long story short, the email said that her son came home in tears because he was not able to go to a party for students who had received both honor roll and exemplary or satisfactory marks under citizenship. There was no doubt that academically he was eligible. He had almost all A's with just one B. And behaviorally, he was fine in my class. He certainly had his silly moments, but in general, he buckled down when I needed him to and had a good sense of humor. She recognized that the reason he wasn't going was because of his behavior in music, where he received an unsatisfactory citizenship mark. She was outraged that his hard work and generally good behavior wasn't being rewarded. Her request was for me to override the requirements that my grade level had put in place and let him attend the celebration.

It was a compelling argument, and her not-happy tone came through loud and clear in the email. I could have taken a number of possible actions:

1. Quickly respond and let her know that it is what it is, and he's not going.
2. Respond that he can go.
3. Not respond and hope that it just blows over.
4. Respond that I would look into it and give her time to cool down.

I went with the fourth choice. I wrote back that I appreciated her email and concern and that I would look into the situation to get more details from the music teacher. I promised that I would get back to her within two days with a phone call. I wanted to keep a strong "marriage" with this parent, so good communication was essential. Quickly shutting her down without any sign of consideration for her feelings may have just made her angrier. Letting her son go to the party without consulting the music teacher or my grade level would have been professionally disrespectful, establishing a bad precedent.

And ignoring the situation would not solve anything in the long run. It would only send the message that I didn't care about her concerns.

Giving myself two days to respond proved a wise move. It gave me time to talk to the music teacher and chat more about his concern with the student's behavior. I learned that the major concern was about responsibility. He frequently forgot his recorder and then lost a recorder he had borrowed from the teacher. It also gave the parent time to cool down. I called her after two days and was greeted with a much different tone than the one expressed in the email. She even apologized for the tone of the email and admitted that she was simply upset because her son was so visibly distraught.

I explained to mom that I had spoken to the music teacher and the issue her son had with responsibility in that class. Since there were no grades in music class, the only place to express the problem was under the citizenship mark. I told her that I was going to stand by the standard set by the grade level, so he would not be able to attend the party, but I promised her that I would meet with her son the next day to come up with a strategy to help him remember the materials he needed for school. With a cooler head, she was much more receptive than she likely would have been had I shared that information shortly after she sent the original email.

We are human, and it is natural for us to be upset at times. Rationalizing or arguing back when tempers flare usually does not end well. *Time* can be a fantastic friend toward reaching more logical and level-headed decisions.

When faced with a fiery situation, let those involved know you have heard them and that you need time to collect information. This effective strategy will help you maintain the "marriage" between stakeholders and set the bar high for the culture within your limitless school.

NASCAR and Stickers (Abe)

A dynamic way to get the culture of your school moving forward is through the aesthetics—giving students, staff, visitors, and district members something to look at that is positive, motivating, and purposeful.

Each summer at Allen Jay, I am tasked by Dr. Wheat to try to come up with new ways to make our environment more inviting. I remember when I was in the classroom how excited I would get trying to come up with innovative themes and decorations. Now in an administrative role, what I choose can't just be something random that I like. It has to showcase our school-wide vision and motivate everyone. That's the first difficult task. The second challenge is finding the time and resources to make things happen! One summer, I tried to tackle both obstacles at once.

As a visitor to Allen Jay, you walk through two sets of sparkling clean glass doors. Once you pass the second set of doors, you are in our office and hallways. This is a high-traffic area, and it's the first impression visitors, parents, and even students see when they come in the front entrance. Now if you are going for a traditional look, then squeaky-clean glass is the way to go; however, to become a limitless school, I wanted to get creative and go beyond just plain old clean. I needed inspiration, and I knew just where to find it.

I am a big sports fan. When I was a kid, I had a life-size cardboard cutout of basketball greats David Robinson and Charles Barkley. I would get compliments from friends about how cool it was to have life-size versions of NBA players in my own room. My love for sports sparked an *aha* moment as I went through the glass doors one morning. My thought: *Why can't we get cutouts of our scholars made and post them around the school?* That was the idea, but I had to first sell the leadership team that this was a good way to spend money. In the end, with a lot of persuasion, they decided to let me loose on the doors and gave me the money to make it happen. I was so excited! Unfortunately, I had absolutely no idea who could create the cutouts.

I did a Google search and called what seemed like a thousand places. I discovered that the cardboard-cutout business isn't as lucrative as it was when I was a kid in the 90s. Although this saddened me, I wasn't going to let the absence of cutout creators derail me from making the school "pop." Keeping an eye out for inspiration, I noticed that Fathead® stickers, the gigantic adhesive stickers that stick on any surface, were still popular. Another light bulb went off! I still had the same problem, though, because I had no idea who was going to be able to make this happen.

> "The two most powerful warriors are patience and time."
>
> LEO TOLSTOY, RUSSIAN AUTHOR

One day after school, a colleague told me about a friend of his who was traveling out of town to go to a NASCAR race. I have little interest in NASCAR but wanted to politely acknowledge the conversation, so I engaged him by asking some generic racing questions. I was expecting him to talk about Dale Earnhardt Jr. for the next twenty-five minutes. Instead, he told me his friend, Chad, participates in the races because he wraps NASCAR cars. I was intrigued and began to ask questions. Minutes later, I discovered that not only did this friend have a company where he can print large stickers, but he lived seven minutes from the school. And the icing on the cake—his wife was a teacher!

You're probably thinking that everything lined up perfectly. You are halfway correct. It took more than three weeks to nail down a time for a conversation with Chad and his associate. At that point, time was running out to take pictures of students, and I still didn't know if a giant sticker would be in our budget or if he could even make this happen.

The meeting went well, and after pulling out the "educator card" (with which Chad was quite familiar), he agreed to take on the project and work within the school's budget. I sweetened the pot and got the price down even further by getting him to sign up as a registered company with the school system; this would help other schools acquire his services and would promote his name in our area.

My goal was to have the project completed during the summer so when students and parents came back, they would have something awesome and motivating to see: themselves! I took more than 150 pictures of our students during a three-day period. I sent the pictures to Chad, and he measured and selected about sixty-five of the best pictures to turn into giant Fathead decals that we could mount throughout the school.

I was feeling better, but the stress kept coming. Chad has a busy schedule working with NASCAR and other companies, so for the money and the small amount of work that we were offering, we fell to the bottom of his queue. Chad was a true professional and great person to work with, and I completely understand why he took his time with our project. But I had promised the leadership team something big, and I was sweating because open house was one week away— and still no decals.

The stress was worth the wait. It all worked out, and now, every time I come into the school, I get to see two giant door decals of our scholars greeting me. When I open the door, there are dozens more throughout the halls to enjoy. The truth is, there were plenty of times when I didn't think this was going to happen. Once the last sticker had been placed onto the wall, I had four months invested into the idea. That's four months of worry, planning, and sweaty palms!

When you are working with local businesses and organizations to make your school a better place, you have to give yourself plenty of time. Invest in patience. Although we may want things to happen overnight, the best things happen over time. Time allowed me to build a relationship with Chad. If I would have rushed him and shown how anxious I was, that may have put a bad taste in his mouth about working with our school and compromised future partnerships.

We've become so accustomed to eggshell-colored walls covering our schools that we've forgotten that we're serving children each day. Kids deserve color, pictures, and a sense of belonging. To become a limitless school, take the time to make your school environment aesthetically inviting. It takes time to get the right people on board, and it takes time and patience to see it through.

What if we were all to use our time to create moments for each other? A moment to celebrate a friend. A moment to give a hug. A moment to say thank you. School culture can be defined through the moments in time that we create and remember.

ABE & ADAM

6

LIMELIGHT

n 2015, star high school English teacher Ruby Ruhf took her teaching talents from Ohio back to New York City's PS 431 in a lucrative, record-setting deal that "awarded her an $80 million guaranteed contract over the next six years, plus an additional $40 million in incentives based on test scores." The move sent shock waves through the teaching community and headlined almost every news publication. Advertisers battled over her endorsement as she was the hottest commodity in the world of education.

If you just chuckled a little or perhaps rolled your eyes, it's because this was clearly not a real story. It comes from the brilliant work of comedians Key and Peele when they produced *TeachingCenter*, a satirical video that featured stories on the nation's best teachers. A spin-off of ESPN's *SportsCenter*, Key and Peele wanted to show a

"Stay true in the dark, and humble in the spotlight."

HAROLD B. LEE, AMERICAN RELIGIOUS LEADER AND EDUCATOR

world where teachers and education were thrust into the spotlight, earning the kind of fame, fortune, and benefits that professional athletes receive today. By the way, if you have never seen the video, we strongly urge you to go to YouTube and type in "Key and Peele TeachingCenter."[1]

Unfortunately, our society is not yet to the point where teachers and schools are on the same level as professional athletes, singers, actors, or the newest trend, "social media stars." We do, however—with the hard work and innovation that goes on each and every day in our schools—have plenty of opportunities to get our schools into the spotlight.

Why is it important to put our schools in the limelight in the first place? As we mentioned in the Introduction, when a spotlight is thrust upon something, others are interested in learning more about it. While we know schools exist in our communities, how much do we really know about them? Could you name the principals of all the schools in your area? Do you know the students' and teachers' needs? Do you know what kinds of remarkable things the teachers are doing?

When stakeholders become more aware and knowledgeable about the schools in their communities and across the country, opportunities for our teachers and students will improve. We have seen this happen when teachers who have large social media followings use their platforms to recognize their schools, colleagues, and, most importantly, their students. As a result, businesses, philanthropists,

---

1 *Comedy Central.* "Key & Peele – TeachingCenter," YouTube, Jul 28, 2015. https://www.youtube.com/watch?v=dkHqPFbxmOU.

and in some cases, celebrities, choose to support and reward those educators and students for the hard work that they do.

Putting your school in the limelight is not about boasting or tooting your own horn. It's about celebrating education and shining a positive light on teachers, schools, and students. When the limelight is on education, we all benefit from new ideas and innovations that can then be passed along to benefit our schools. Remember, *we're all in this together!*

THE STATE SUPERINTENDENT VISITS (ABE)

Newly elected North Carolina state school superintendent had heard good things about Allen Jay through the grapevine, but he wanted to see things for himself. One of his advisors contacted the school and set up the visit. At Allen Jay, visitors are always welcome, but it's not every day that the state superintendent wants to come hang out at your school!

With most visitations, we select scholars to help us greet guests. We also choose a grade level to perform any content songs or activities that they are currently doing in their classrooms. This is a way to highlight students, teachers, and staff members while they share their innovative ideas and skills.

We knew that having an influential individual, especially one who can impact policy, come to our school provided an opportunity to bring a positive light to our school and to education in general. It offered the chance to show this guest the culture of our school and why people are talking about it. We also felt the weight of the underlying responsibility to be an ambassador for educational reform.

To get the ball rolling, the administrative team notified news outlets and our Allen Jay families. A few parents responded that they wanted to help provide breakfast treats and coffee upon the superintendent's arrival. This set the stage for him because he was able to talk to parents and get their perspective of the school through their eyes.

A school district board member also caught wind that the state superintendent was coming and wanted to be a part of the visit. It turned out that she was an alumnus of Allen Jay when it was a high school back in the 1960s. This was particularly intriguing because she was able to give the superintendent her viewpoint of the school as an alumnus, school board member, and parent of children who went through public education.

We wanted to ensure that he saw the possibilities of what a school can do. It was our hope that his experience and takeaways could influence his position on issues that come across his table as state superintendent that would benefit schools statewide.

Sometimes you get lucky, and the state superintendent wants to stop by. Other times, you have to create a little magic as a staff member, parent, or district official and call members of the community and news outlets to come see your school and the awesome things that you are doing. Positive press helps boost your staff morale, overall culture, and the perspective in which the community views your school; it validates what you are doing and encourages stakeholders to work even harder. By the way, we were thrilled that the superintendent's scheduled one-hour visit turned into an almost three-hour stay!

FACEBOOK REVIEW (ABE)

Many schools are moving toward using social media to allow outsiders to get an inside look on what the school is all about. If used correctly, social media can be a powerful tool to help put your school in the limelight and build a culture of inspiration by highlighting teachers, students, events, and awards. Allen Jay chose, from the beginning, to get on board with Facebook. We thought that posting videos, pictures, and comments via Facebook would be the best platform for our school. When you create a business or community organization page on Facebook, you give the public an opportunity to rate your school. This can be a helpful tool because it provides instant feedback on what visitors think.

I learned early on that you will always have someone who doesn't like what you are doing, and that goes for anything in life. My dad always told me it's how you respond in those situations that defines your integrity and who you are as a person.

I was fiddling through Facebook one evening after an awards ceremony to check out all the pictures that were taken at the event. I couldn't help but notice that someone left the school a "one-star" rating and a negative review.

The negative review, which was based on our football team, came from a gentleman who has a niece at our school. To be honest, it seemed a bit out of left field. The thing was, it wasn't even that the comment was degrading or harsh; it was just confusing. It read: "My

"Cultivate the habit of being grateful for every good thing that comes to you, and to give thanks continuously. And because all things have contributed to your advancement, you should include all things in your gratitude."

RALPH WALDO EMERSON, AMERICAN POET

niece attends this school and the football coach doesn't do a good job on the field with his players. He is always yelling at them, not who I want coaching my kids." This comment was odd for a couple reasons. First, our football coach has never had any complaints come his way on his coaching or treatment of players. Second, this person has never even stepped foot inside of our school building. But if your school is in the limelight, and as you work to be a limitless school, you open yourself up to all sorts of critiques and comments.

As I contemplated responding, I saw a reply pop up, then another, and another. It wasn't me doing the replying; it was three parents from our school. They weren't harsh in their replies but stood firm in reassuring the complainer what our school was about, the things their children had learned, and how they have grown so much while being at Allen Jay. I was proud of those parents. Then a few more replies started pouring in. This time, they came from students! In what would normally be a nerve-racking experience, having students respond on social media to a negatively charged parent, the students came across as mature and level-headed. They echoed what their parents had already said and added in an even more personal perspective.

Even with a great culture, your limitless school is still open to criticism. It is important to respect that people have the right to their point of view and may see things differently. In this instance, it was inspiring to see parents and students stand up for their school and do so in a respectful and proud manner.

SCHOOL SWAG

Next time you are out on the town—at a mall, the movies, a restaurant, or just walking down the street—take note of any signs of "school swag." Do people in your community support their local schools by wearing or showing school pride? Are people proud to wear their school colors or display their mascot?

One of our favorite ways to demonstrate school pride is through visuals. It's fairly common to walk around cities and see signs of professional sport teams or college letters. Have you ever been in Pittsburgh on a Sunday in December? There's a good chance you will come across people waving black and gold flags in support of their Pittsburgh Steelers. Or in our state of North Carolina, it's natural to see people walking around with the letters UNC (University of North Carolina) pasted across their chests (which pains us, by the way, since we both went to rival colleges of UNC's).

Wearing or displaying school or team pride shows solidarity and commitment to a common cause, and when that cause is school, it helps shine a limelight that stakeholders use to spark conversations, network, and ultimately build stronger culture. What follows is a series of ideas for expanding your "school swag" culture:

- Create a school store that sells clothing, book bags, school supplies, lanyards, electronic-device covers, umbrellas, water bottles, flash drives, mugs, etc., with your school's name or logo on it.
- Provide free car bumper magnets to every family at the school. Encourage parents to put them on their car to raise awareness about the school.
- Have school-spirit days where students are encouraged to wear clothing with the school's name or colors.
- Connect with local restaurants to create a spirit night, where students who show up wearing a shirt with the school's name get a discount or free dessert.
- Connect with a local college to get free tickets to an athletic event and have all the kids wear a shirt with the school's name.
- In school districts with a larger number of schools, have a contest to show the most school pride during Homecoming week. The contest can run through a social media outlet like Twitter, using a common hashtag.

At Allen Jay, we decided to invest in something for scholars that they could buy at a great price but also enjoy and promote our school at the same time. There was only one option: Allen Jay socks! Wearing mid-high socks with your slick shoes is the current fashion trend, so why not be a part of it? We ordered white and pink mid-high socks and had our school logo printed on them. We knew that they would sell with the kids, but we didn't realize what a hit they'd become! On dress-down days at our school, it's cool to see our kids sporting the AJ Prep socks around the school. And it's even better to hear stories from over the weekend about kids wearing the socks at their basketball games or out and about. Not only do the kids love them, but they have proven to be a great way to market our school and start conversations.

School swag is common at the middle and high school level, often due to the presence of sports. We encourage and challenge elementary schools to push the presence of school swag as well to help ingrain the concept of school pride at an early age. We would love to see your school pride! Use the hashtag #LimitlessSchool and post a picture of your school swag on social media.

MEDIA COVERAGE (ADAM)

I co-founded a math organization called ROCKmath with my good friend and math teacher extraordinaire, Dr. Camille Jones. ROCKmath's tagline is "Teach like a math star," and it shines positive light on mathematics and on amazing teachers. Too often, great teaching gets tucked away in our schools and classrooms. If we're to grow our profession and put a positive light on education, we need to find ways for the public to know about what's going on inside of the building!

To put these teachers in the limelight, Camille and I came up with a contest called the "ROCKmath Classroom Takeover," where teachers explain or show how they "rock math" in their classrooms. The winner would have Camille and me come to their school to rock math with their students for the day. We have held this contest a couple of times, and our two winners, Ms. Johnson from Florida and Mr. Ipock from Kentucky, both demonstrated a passion for not only math but also for teaching in general.

Because we believe that it's important for great teachers to be celebrated beyond their classroom walls, Camille and I were excited to see that local media came out to cover the story on the day we showed up to do our classroom takeover days. The media presence gave us an opportunity to show the great things these teachers are doing and to shine a limelight directly on their schools.

"You can raise the bar, or you can wait for others to raise it, but it's getting raised regardless."

SETH GODIN, AMERICAN AUTHOR

Tip *Local news outlets truly enjoy showing the positive things going on in our schools, so it's up to us to make sure that they know that there are great things going on!*

Another instance in which media helped spread positive vibes about a school happened in Nebraska. I had been asked to conduct a day of professional development for a school system early on in the school year. From what I was told, some parents in the community were upset that the students had a day off just a couple weeks into the semester. Thinking proactively, administrators at the central office made sure that the community understood the value of the day for the teachers in the district. The professional development coordinator called the local media outlets and asked that they come cover the event and show it was going to positively impact teaching and learning. We had the newspaper, radio, and television stations all there, and they each produced pieces on the purpose for that day. The media helped put a positive spotlight on the district and its teachers by showcasing the great things that they were looking to do.

> *Tip* *If you have a big event or project at your school or school system, don't be afraid to call your local newspaper, news, or radio station. Forming relationships with the local media allows them to paint a picture of our schools for the community that positively influences stakeholders' views of our schools.*

WE AND US

Do you know someone who only talks about their own achievements and life every time you come into contact with him? Think about words you'd use to describe that person and how that person makes you feel. Being in the limelight is a great thing for a school, but as teachers and leaders, we each need to be careful not to become "that person"—the one who always talks about themselves and fails to acknowledge the collaborative effort that creates success in our schools. Personally, we feel blessed to have had opportunities to work at schools that have been in the limelight. Through both of our experiences, we have learned that, while it is an honor to work at a school that is highlighted, it's also important to remain humble and grateful when you are receiving the attention.

> *Tip* *Talking about your team, the students, and the collaborative process at your school is one way to enjoy the limelight while remaining humble. Whenever you have visitors and guests at your school, it's important to use a lot of "we" and "us" to talk about your school. Using "I" and "me" may be negatively perceived.*

One of the biggest questions I (Abe) get when people visit Allen Jay is, "What do you guys do when the cameras aren't here?" I used to brush off that question because I thought it was an attack, but over time, I've realized it really is a fair question. Why *wouldn't* people suspect the picture they see is "just for show"? Visitors, district officials, parents, and other district teachers weren't asking this question to be rude; they truly wanted to know how the culture of expectations stayed high even after the cameras and visitors left. My answer has and will always remain the same: At Allen Jay, all staff members expect excellence from all of our scholars, regardless of the day of the week and regardless of who is in the building. Our scholars understand this and rise to the occasion. Even when I answer that question, I don't say, "I expect," I say, "We expect." That language of unity sets the tone and lets visitors know that the staff members at our school are on the same page.

KEEP RAISING THE BAR

When a school experiences a lot of positive press, it isn't uncommon for its staff and students to get comfortable with their results and lose their hunger and drive.

Our first fifth-grade class came to the school with a little over 30 percent proficiency in math and reading. Three years later, those students are over 70 percent proficient as a group. We will celebrate this because it is a wonderful accomplishment and a testament to the hard work from all stakeholders, but we will also spend our summer looking for ways to move the next group to 80 percent, 90 percent, and so on. The expectation of continual improvement creates a culture of hunger and drive. Don't get me wrong, there are definitely times to pause and celebrate and give credit where it is deserved. Just don't party on the sidelines for too long. Get back out there and push for the next win!

Lastly, remember that the limelight doesn't last forever. If you are getting positive press as a school, enjoy it. Make the most of that exposure and work to find creative ways to keep it going. If you are out and about in town and you overhear someone say the name of your school, jump in and introduce yourself and speak positively about your experience. Whenever you bring up your job, students, or school district, be humble but show your pride. You may not be comfortable simply jumping into conversations and speaking to strangers, but building your limitless school requires an uncommon approach. If nothing else, wear your school swag and be an ambassador of excellence!

The true fuel of the limelight is people who care. How can you add fuel to your school's illumination?

ABE & ADAM

7

EDUCATE YOURSELF

We're about to expose ourselves a bit here: We know that we are both highly privileged. Not in the traditional sense. Neither one of us come from or possess great financial wealth, but we're privileged in a different way. We are both *white, heterosexual, able-bodied males*. Over the course of time, our society has associated privilege with certain groups of people. By definition, when someone is privileged, another group is not.

Don't believe us?

Neither of us have to worry about people questioning the legality of our marriages. I (Adam) had a former colleague who went to a neighboring state to marry his partner (this was before the Supreme Court ruled that same-sex marriages were legal in all states). When he returned to our state, he was questioned by some on how he was able to marry his partner.

Neither of us have to worry for our safety when we come face-to-face with law enforcement. When I (Abe) was once pulled over for going thirty miles over the speed limit, I was given a warning by the police officer and went on my way. My African-American colleague at work was once handcuffed (for the officer's safety, it was explained) during a traffic stop for what the cop said was a broken taillight.

Neither of us have to worry about people underselling our qualifications. My (Adam) wife is a pediatrician, and at least once a week, she comes home with a story about how a patient or patient's family will assume that she is their nurse, and they'll save their questions "for the doctor."

You get the point.

The funny thing about having privilege is you don't always realize you have it. You don't question many things in your day-to-day life because they're usually in your favor. We were both born into these privileges, and it's taken us into our professional lives before we realized that the most important part of having privilege is being an ally to those who don't. You'll see examples of this in our stories that follow.

When building the limitless school, each individual—regardless of gender, race, sexuality, or ability—must have a platform from which to speak. We are all unique. We all have stories to tell. It's through the personal experiences that we each bring to the table that we build trust, empathy, and understanding for one another. A positive school culture can be built around those traits, and it's up to stakeholders to ensure that each person feels safe and welcomed to share their story.

Phi Delta Part II (Adam)

Earlier in the book, you learned about Phi Delta, a middle school fraternity I created to provide mentorship and role models for a group of eighth-grade students at a local middle school. For one of our first activities, I brought the Wake Forest University baseball team to do a variety of activities with the students. The students loved having a group of college-aged student athletes join them for the morning. Afterward, Javian, one of the eighth-grade boys came up to me and said, "Mr. D., that was cool; can you bring a basketball player too?"

I told him I could invite a basketball player to a meeting, but I was curious as to why he had wanted a basketball player specifically, so I asked him. I expected him to say something along the lines of "basketball is more fun," or "I play basketball."

> "Knowledge is power. Information is liberating. Education is the premise of progress, in every society, in every family."
>
> KOFI ANNAN, GHANAIAN DIPLOMAT

Instead, he responded, "Well, there was only one black dude on that baseball team."

I thought about his reasoning, and while I suppose I realized there was only one non-Caucasian person on the baseball team, I hadn't thought about how that spoke to the students. Now it may have been a flawed assumption on Javian's part to think that all basketball players are black, but his point was well taken. In these students' minds, these athletes were "cool" because they played baseball, but aside from one player, none of those college students looked like them. Javian's comment was a reality check for me. I thought, *If I am trying to provide positive role models for these students, almost all of whom are African-American or Hispanic, how credible is a group of Caucasian college students to them?*

That conversation with Javian influenced my recruitment for a future activity to which I invited the brothers of the Alpha Phi Alpha Fraternity, a historically black Greek organization, to meet the boys. Their eyes lit up as four confident, sharply dressed black men wearing their Greek-lettered jackets walked in the room. For the first time, I saw Andrew not goofing around when someone else was talking. For the first time, I saw Berto participate and be successful when he step-danced. And for the first time, I saw Shamar smile.

When we consider ways to reach our students through role models, we should be mindful of the people our students look up to. Talking to students and listening to what they say can provide an education into who they would be interested in learning from. It is our job to weed through their idols and decide who embodies the character traits we want our students to emulate. From there, we can seek out books students can read, videos for them to watch, or opportunities in the community that allow them to connect with positive role models.

"The function of education is to teach one to think intensively and to think critically. Intelligence plus character—that is the goal of true education."

MARTIN LUTHER KING, JR., AMERICAN CIVIL RIGHTS LEADER AND ACTIVIST

The United Nations (Adam)

One of my fondest teaching memories came while working at Endhaven Elementary School in Charlotte, North Carolina. It was open house night. The students and families came in, excited to meet their new teachers and see their classrooms. It was my first year at the school, so I was a mystery to these families, and they were unknown to me. There's always an element of anxiousness as you prepare for the arrival of the families. Any teacher can tell you that you want to make a great first impression on these nights, and smiling for two hours is no easy task!

As the clock struck 5:00 p.m. and the doors to the school opened, I welcomed the new families into my room. During the next couple of hours, I put faces with names, and noticed that, as I met family after family, my new students each had unique stories and backgrounds:

- Aaron (his English name) and his family had just arrived in the United States about a week prior from South Korea and did not speak any English. The dad had a pre-translated note that he gave me that explained the situation. The note said that he was excited for his son to be at the school.
- Nelli's family was Iranian, and she was fluent in English and Farsi.
- Lina's family was Lebanese, and they promised me that they would fatten me up by the end of the year by feeding me all sorts of Lebanese food.
- Asuka and her family had lived in the United States and Japan because of her dad's job. Asuka and her father were fluent in Japanese and English, but her mother spoke only Japanese.
- Gina's family was Mexican, and she is bilingual.
- Alan's family is Chinese-American, and his parents are bilingual.

After meeting these families, I knew it would be a year unlike any other I had experienced. Sitting in front of me was a kaleidoscope of cultures, religions, races, and backgrounds. It was as if I had my own mini United Nations right in front of me. To capitalize on this opportunity, however, I needed to learn more about each of my students, their families, and their rich and varied cultures. That year, I spent time talking to the students at lunch, recess, or during downtime about customs they have at home. I wanted to make sure that my teaching reflected culturally relevant pedagogy that made all learners feel welcome.

When it came time for my annual Cultural Cookout that year, a yearly reading unit I did with my fifth graders, I had the most amazing culinary contributions from families! For this unit, I always asked families to bring in a food sample from either the culture of the book that the students had read or something from their own heritage. Traditionally, I've had families bring in *matzah* or *challah* bread if the student read Number the Stars, or burritos if they read The Circuit. That year, though, we had hummus and falafel from Lina's family, *baghali polo* (a dish with rice and bean) from Nelli's family, and an assortment of other homemade dishes that the parents were so proud to cook and share as a representation of their backgrounds.

It is often said that our students teach us as much as, if not more than, we teach them. That year, I can honestly say I was educated, not just from the standpoint of learning about different cultures, but how to build a classroom culture that embraces different individuals and families. When we provide opportunities to learn about one another, we lay the foundation for a school culture that embraces diversity of thought, race, religion, and sexuality.

MARTA (ADAM)

During my time working at the Ron Clark Academy, some individuals came to the school each year to attend our educator training. The training allows visitors to observe teachers at work in their classrooms. A few people came multiple times during the school year. Typically, the repeat guests were principals or district-level folks who were bringing in different groups each time. As a staff, we got to know many of these individuals personally.

One person whom I had the pleasure of interacting with many times was Superintendent Bill McAllister ("Mr. Mac"). Mr. Mac came to us from rural eastern Nebraska where the closest airport was hours away. I learned from my conversations with Mr. Mac that his goal was always for his teachers to "see more." Many of the families in his community grew up there and remained there, generation after generation. He knew his teachers could learn by seeing other schools, and he chose the Ron Clark Academy in Atlanta as a destination for every single one of the teachers in his district during his time as superintendent.

The reason Mr. Mac's story is in this chapter is because of what he did when he arrived in Atlanta with his groups. First, you should know that the Ron Clark Academy is in the Lakewood Heights neighborhood of southeast Atlanta, which is a predominately African-American area. Mr. Mac's district, at the time, was 99 percent white. In fact, one of my former colleagues at Ron Clark Academy, Mr. Townsel, once went to Mr. Mac's district to conduct professional development. Townsel told me after the visit that he was the talk of the town—many of the folks there had never met a black man before!

When Mr. Mac brought his group to Atlanta, the only way his teachers were allowed to travel around was via MARTA, the city's public transportation system. Imagine being an adult who has lived in a small town all your life where there is a good chance you know most (if not all) of the people in your community, and suddenly being thrust into a gigantic city where there are more people on the train at that moment than perhaps in your whole town. Mr. Mac knew that the only way his teachers would grow professionally and personally was by being exposed to new experiences, even if they were uncomfortable.

I got to speak with many of his teachers as they came through the school, and they always had such gratitude toward Mr. Mac for pushing them to do something new. Many had never been on a plane, train, or bus before. Further, many had never interacted with a person of a different ethnicity and were now taking public transportation into a predominantly minority neighborhood and spending the day with a majority African-American student population.

Mr. Mac's vision and mission to grow his teachers is admirable and deserving of a story. He had the means as superintendent to make it happen and showed leadership by traveling to Atlanta each time to show his staff that he was going to be just as much a part of the change as they were. He designed a limitless school system that practiced what it preached!

LEARNING ABOUT YOURSELF (ABE)

While we have focused on how to educate yourself through your work and through those with whom you surround yourself, there are moments when it is equally important to educate yourself about *yourself*. My wife, Brittany, grew up in Noblesville, Indiana, a suburb of Indianapolis and a great place to raise a family. Each time we visit, I am always astonished that people leave their doors unlocked at night because of the tight-knit communities in Noblesville. Life and opportunities haven't always been perfect for Brittany, however; she experienced eye-opening insights about society as a child. Brittany has an African-American dad and a white mom. Although interracial marriage numbers have risen dramatically during the past decade, some places still aren't as accepting as others.

Brittany grew up mixed in a predominantly white area. As she gained life experience, she became increasingly more inquisitive about who she was and the story of her African-American heritage, partly because it was less pronounced in her community. When attempting to learn more about her African-American side, however, she found challenges trying to fit in with single-race groups. Her African-American peers shunned her from conversations for not being "black enough." White peers cast her off as not being "white enough," putting her in an awkward place.

Brittany has shared stories with me about how her blended ethnicity has affected her life. She remembers riding in the car with her dad and being pulled over by police officers for "unreasonable" things. She remembers people looking at her and her family differently when they would go to places together. When Brittany and I first started dating in 2013, I took her to a BBQ joint. I remember the stares we received while eating. I had never before been so conscious of my skin color. It was the first time, but not the last, that I really got a glimpse into some of the challenges that my wife faced personally and academically based on her skin color.

Brittany has spent a large portion of her life educating herself about herself. We have students in our schools who face similar challenges. They fight prejudice and confusion in their own identity to truly learn who they are. Any number of reasons

> "Education is not preparation for life; education is life itself."
>
> John Dewey, American Education Reformist and Philosopher

can lead to a student feeling uncomfortable in their own skin, and it is important in a limitless school to find resources and mentors to help these individuals feel comfortable and welcomed in our schools.

WAYS TO EDUCATE YOURSELF

We believe one key to educating yourself is having the desire to be educated. An open mind and open heart are good places to start. When you are ready to educate yourself, there are three concrete ways you can begin the process:

1. **Become a lifelong learner.** Stay abreast of current issues and research. Read the works of Gloria Ladson-Billings, Geneva Gay, and Allan Johnson, to name a few. Their stories will enlighten you on important perspectives regarding cultural competency and privilege. Attend conferences and professional development that discuss ways to be an upstander, an activist, or a more informed citizen. Bring speakers to your schools who have experience in diverse situations or have a story they are willing to tell. In addition to the topics we've looked at above, discussions on immigration and LGBTQ issues are relevant and pressing right now in our schools, and it is important to be informed on these subjects.

2. **Put yourself in uncomfortable situations.** Visit places you would not normally go. Engage with people who are different than you. Talk with them about their lives and share your story. Join conversations with people of different viewpoints. It's easy to find ways you're different, but challenge yourself to find ways that you're alike. Work with children who are challenging and defiant. Listen to them.

3. **Find avenues to be an ally.** When necessary, stand alongside those less privileged to show solidarity and support. Join movements and rallies that support positive change. Fight

for education and schools and particularly for students who have traditionally been marginalized. Support families that want the best for their children but may not have the means to make it happen.

To close the chapter, we'd like to each share one more story about a way we've educated ourselves in our professional careers.

RELIGIOUS AWAKENING (ADAM)

I did not grow up with religion as an important part of my life. While my father was raised Catholic and my mother was raised Jewish, our household did not embrace any one religious affiliation. I certainly have nothing against religion, and it is a large part of many of my friends' lives, so I always respect their views as they do mine. With that being said, I am clearly a novice when it comes to any type of experience surrounding places of worship.

So it was apropos that the year that I had my "United Nations" class, I also had my first two personal invites to places of worship with my students. The first came from one of my young ladies, Lana. She and her family invited me to their temple for a special service. At that point, the only time I had ever been to a temple was for my cousin's *bar mitzvah* about fifteen years prior. Apparently, I had mentioned to Lana that my mom was Jewish at some point because I got the feeling there was an expectation that I knew what I was doing when I got there. Needless to say, I did not, but I worked my hardest to keep up with the songs and rituals! We ended up having a fantastic time, and the look on Lana's face every time she got to introduce me to one of the people there was worth it.

The second invite came from one of my young men, Joey. Joey and his family invited me to his brother's christening at their church. Being fairly unfamiliar with how the christening procedures work, I closely watched other people to see what they did, and I tried my best to not make a fool of myself during prayers. Luckily, the focus was on Joey's brother, so I was able to blend in quite easily at that event. The family was so grateful to have me there, and I took the experience as a great awakening to my education!

With both of these invites, honestly, my initial gut reaction was to decline and say I was busy. I had convinced myself that I would be uncomfortable and awkward in these places. Instead, I reminded myself that I am a learner, and that to grow, I needed to be willing step outside my comfort zone. I ask my students to push themselves every day and take on new experiences, so how could I not do the same?

Boundaries for Kids (Abe)

Over the years, I have worked hard to find ways to engage with parents beyond traditional meet and greets. I strive to get to know families' successes and struggles so I can better reach their child at school. This can, at times, be challenging because it calls for delving into personal lives, which some families wish to remain private.

At Allen Jay, we make every effort to meet the needs of our parents. Even so, I realized that we weren't learning a lot about them personally. My principal, Dr. Wheat, had an idea one year to cultivate a book study with our parents. He purchased books through a grant and gave copies to parents during open house. The book was titled *Boundaries for Kids* and is a compilation of research and best practices for raising your child into their teenage years.

Now, we didn't brand this as the holy grail of all books, and we didn't give it to parents at open house and say, "Read this or else." It was simply packaged as a resource and a way to open the lines of communication between the school and parents on what practices work best for raising children who want to be successful and lifelong learners.

Every few weeks, my principal sent out an email to parents giv-ing them updates and reminders for things to come, and at the very bottom, he would review a few chapters of the book and list a few open-ended questions. What was great about the questions is that parents would respond back with their opinion and ask questions of their own. When we saw parents at ball games, they often mentioned something they had read in the book or a strategy that was eye-open-ing for them. The book opened up an avenue for conversations that allowed parents to safely communicate any frustrations or successes that they were experiencing with their children at home. The best part is that, over time, the dialogue changed from just being about school to being more about how the school and home can be consis-tent in their practices.

Not every parent participated, and not every parent who read the book ever engaged us in conversation about it. However, it opened the door to open and honest communication with parents and teachers alike on the need to educate ourselves on best practices for raising children.

Education comes when you
become comfortable in
what was an uncomfortable
situation.

ABE & ADAM

8

SUCCESS

You may have never heard of Dan Syrek, but there's a good chance you are familiar with his work. Ever heard of the phrase, "Don't mess with Texas"? In the 1980s, the Lone Star State was spending tens of millions of dollars a year cleaning up roadside litter. They brought in Syrek and his team, leading researchers on litter, to help fix the problem. Texas had previously attempted anti-litter campaigns through commercials that appealed to sympathetic citizens. "Give a Hoot—Don't Pollute" was a catchy phrase, but it didn't appeal to the state's guiltiest parties, the group of rough, tough men Syrek collectively called "Bubba."

With this realization, Syrek and his team created a campaign to appeal to "Bubba" by showcasing people to whom "Bubba" could relate. They featured famous Texans like football legends Ed "Too Tall" Jones and Randy White, baseball pitcher Mike Scott, boxer

"Success is not final; failure is not fatal; it is the courage to continue that counts."

WINSTON CHURCHILL, BRITISH
PRIME MINISTER

George Foreman, blues guitarist Stevie Ray Vaughan, and country singer Willie Nelson. In each of the ads, these Texan heroes were tasked with shaking their fists at people littering and sharing, in their deep voices, that familiar phrase, "Don't mess with Texas."

The campaign worked. Within the first few months, 73 percent of Texans polled could recall the message. Within a year, litter had declined 29 percent. Within five years of the campaign, visible roadside litter in Texas decreased 72 percent, and the number of cans along Texas roads dropped 81 percent.

This story and many others are shared in an incredibly impactful book called *Made to Stick: Why Some Ideas Survive and Others Die* by brothers Chip and Dan Heath.[1] This is not a book about education per se, but everything included in it can easily be brought back to improving our school culture. If we use the models included in *Made to Stick*, such as "Don't Mess with Texas," as a guide, we can deem a school's culture shift a success when *it sticks*.

Appropriately, the Heath brothers use the acronym "SUCCESs" to help explain ways in which things stick. Things that are Simple, Unexpected, Concrete, Credible, Emotional, and utilize Stories are "stickier" and more provoking. Thinking back to what we have talked about so far in the limitless school, the ways in which you can build your school culture almost always involve SUCCESs.

1 Heath, Chip, and Dan Heath, *Made to Stick: Why Some Ideas Survive and Others Die*. New York: Random House, 2010.

Building culture through ensuring a guest in your school is welcomed with a smile is simple. Starting the new school year off with giant decals of the students hanging around the school is unexpected. Using the Rubik's Cube as a metaphor for our stakeholders coming together makes the concept concrete. Having parents or students write heartfelt testimonies about your school draws upon credibility, emotion, and stories all at once.

As we work to build a positive culture in our limitless schools, it's necessary and appropriate to occasionally stop and measure our progress. Because it can be challenging, at times, to attach a number or percentage to something as abstract as culture, we believe that the true test of impactful school culture is when it sticks. If you're wondering whether your culture shifts have stuck, ask yourself the following questions:

Are the practices we have put in place sustainable?

When the current teachers, parents, administrators, and students are gone, is there a positive culture that remains?

The measuring stick for a successful school culture is when long-lasting, meaningful impact touches every side of the culture cube.

TRADITIONS

Imagine that you're at your high school reunion and have a chance to meet current students at your alma mater. As you engage in conversation about "the good old days" and talk about some of your fondest memories at the school, the young lady you're talking to happily tells you those practices are still in place. Culture thrives on traditions. The ability to pass traditions from one generation to the next demonstrates success in school culture.

Establishing or keeping traditions alive is important to the people involved at the school. It is a means for attracting alumni back in and re-engaging folks who may have been gone for many years. Going back to your elementary school twenty years later and hearing the students sing the same school song you once did brings back fond memories. In turn, having this connection with the school encourages individuals to want to support the school now.

I (Adam) attended a school fair in my district where schools each had a table and were recruiting new families to their school. One of the middle schools had a group of about a dozen alumni who were now college students or professionals representing their school and talking to perspective families about how this school made a difference in their lives. What great credibility that experience made on the parents trying to decide whether to send their child to this middle school!

There are a number of fun traditions that schools across the country maintain that we'd like to share:

- **Graduate Walks**: During graduation season at high schools, seniors return to their elementary schools to walk in their caps and gowns down their elementary school hallways as current students clap and give high-fives.

- **Big Friend–Little Friend** (mentor program): When students start a new school, they are assigned a "big friend" (mentor) who helps them adjust to the school. As they move to the upper grades, they then become a big friend and receive a little friend.

- **Independence Day**: It can be intimidating for kindergartners to start school, so it may be customary for parents to walk their children to class. At Vienna Elementary, where Adam used to work, they have Independence Day, where on day ten of school, the entire school wears red, white, and blue clothing. It marks the official first day where kindergartners have to walk to class without any parents.

- **Handprints**: Upon graduation each year, many schools have found ways for graduates to leave a lasting mark. One form of remembrance is a handprint. Using a hallway or stairwell, have the graduates that year leave their handprint and write their name or initials under it. How cool will that be for those students to return to the school many years later and find their handprints!

- **Class Rock**: Some schools have giant boulders in front of their school, and it becomes tradition for the graduating class that year to paint the rock and decorate it for the community to see.

We encourage you to reflect upon the traditions that exist in your school and consider how you can ensure they remain alive. A successful culture respects and maintains the school's positive traditions. If your school is new or does not have any defined traditions, there's no better time to start one! Brainstorm ideas with stakeholders and try to make your new idea *stick*.

BACK TO FERTITTA (ADAM)

Earlier in this book, you learned about Principal Lisa Burkhead and her efforts to turn Fertitta Middle School into a five-star school. Lisa has since moved on to lead a high school, but I have had a chance to return to Fertitta under the new administration. I was so pleased to see that the culture Lisa and her team built remained strong. As I walked through the halls, students shook my hand, held the door open for me, and naturally responded with, "Yes, sir." Students stand to respond when they answer a question and start off by introducing themselves to the guests in the room. During my meetings with the staff, the staff members who spoke also stood and introduced themselves to me, modeling a consistency in expectations they have for students.

There may have been fear that teachers and staff would go back to old routines once Lisa left, but the expectations she established had become so ingrained in the culture of Fertitta that it's simply part of who they are now. The new principal at the school, Dr. Ellis, respected the work and efforts that went into raising the bar at Fertitta and has worked to maintain the culture while continuing to push them to become even better.

In measuring the success of Fertitta's school culture, the way that positive habits have stuck—even after leaders have changed and students have graduated—demonstrates the mark of outstanding work. Fertitta's culture cube has been aligned, stakeholders are speaking the same language, and they are continuing to push further and are finding new ways to advance their limitless school.

THE NUMBERS

While we did mention that it's hard to put a number on establishing school culture, we believe there are a handful of quantitative indicators that can give insight into your progress. When meeting as a school, a school leadership team, central office, or PTA, it's certainly reasonable to use data to guide discussions about your school's culture. What follows are examples of measures that we feel are appropriate to use when you are evaluating your efforts in building or improving school culture.

Surveys

In our state of North Carolina, we have the Teacher Working Conditions Survey (ncteachingconditions.org) that every public school in the state completes every other year. Teachers and staff at the school are asked to evaluate a series of statements that inquire about protected time, facilities and resources, community support and involvement, teacher and administrative leadership, and so on. The results are collected, and schools are expected to use the data to guide discussions on school improvement.

A strong leader will use these results to evaluate culture change and lead discussions on next steps. For example, one statement reads, "There is an atmosphere of trust and mutual respect in the school." If only 50 percent "agree" or "strongly agree" with that statement, that implies that half of the staff may not feel respected at work. For leaders, that insight should be concerning. Making respect a topic of discussion moving forward and setting the goal to find ways to build trust are steps that leaders could take to help improve the culture of trust and respect within the school.

Not every state has a uniform survey like North Carolina's, so it is important for district leaders (e.g., superintendents, board of education members, central office administrators) to establish a way for stakeholders like students, teachers, and parents to evaluate their school and provide feedback. Parent surveys offer insight on how a positive school culture is carried into the home. Students who are being taught valuable life skills at school often internalize and then demonstrate those traits outside of school. It's important for parents to provide feedback to the school on the things that are going right as well as on the areas that need improvement.

> "Coming together is a beginning; keeping together is progress; working together is success."
>
> HENRY FORD, AMERICAN BUSINESSMAN

ATTENDANCE

It's quite simple: Kids like going to places they enjoy and feel loved. For certain students, a mild sniffle or hangnail is the only excuse they need to stay home from school. Why? Because it's not a place they love going. So what if we were to create schools where kids loved coming—a place where they looked forward to giving their teacher a hug or handshake, learning through games and engaging lessons, and building relationships with peers?

We believe that creating limitless schools actually helps increase attendance. To gauge the progress of building or improving a school culture, take a look at trends for both student and teacher attendance, especially in comparison to similar time frames in years past.

An elementary school in South Carolina went through a culture transformation after several staff members desired to see a change in their school. One of the issues they were facing was a significant attendance problem. After implementing several culture-changing initiatives, they examined the attendance data and found that compared to prior years, 130 students (out of 408) had perfect attendance during the first 63 days of school.

One year later, after a number of additional practices were put into place, including a "House System," attendance saw a dramatic shift. Students earned points for their House when they had perfect attendance, which was celebrated by the entire school. As a result, the school saw 200 students (out of 423) with perfect attendance during the first quarter. For number junkies, that's about a 15 percent increase in perfect attendance. I know many administrators would enjoy seeing that type of growth in a one-year span.

By examining this data, the school was able to recognize the success of their efforts and to see areas that still needed improvement. For instance, even though perfect attendance went up, overall absenteeism decreased by only a few percentage points. This type of data helped the data team to conclude that a certain group of students caused the majority of the absences. With this information, they could consider initiatives, such as individual outreach to specific families.

Attendance data, when used to measure the success of building and improving a school culture, helps tell the story of your efforts and their impact on students and families.

BEHAVIOR

Student behavior is a frequent topic of discussion among educators and parents because it has a significant impact on the educational experience. Student disruptions can take away teaching time, suspensions can cause rifts between administrators and parents, and office referrals take away time from administrators for doing other things to help the school. In contrast, classrooms and schools with positive student behaviors are frequently more productive, receive better reviews, and are able to attract better teachers. School culture is certainly affected by student behavior.

When office referrals, suspensions, and classroom disruptions become a topic of concern at a school and have a negative impact on school culture, stakeholders must come together to examine data and find the source of the problem; for example, is there a particular group of students, time of day, or classroom that causes the bulk of the issues?

While we can guarantee that behavior challenges will never completely go away (we're dealing with kids after all), having discussions and establishing school-wide norms and procedures for how to deal with behavior issues gives stakeholders clear steps on what to do when problems arise. When people feel supported and confident in dealing with conflicts, morale goes up. This leads to a more positive culture since people are working together versus feeling isolated.

RETENTION

Teacher and student retention is another category we feel is appropriate to examine when measuring the success of your school's culture transformation. First, it is important to note that schools have natural turnover. Teachers and families are human; life happens. People move and experience life changes (e.g., marriage, children, jobs) or other personal circumstances that may require them to leave their school. And sometimes the school is not the right fit for an educator or a family. If someone leaves because it is not the right fit, does that mean the school transformation is a failure? No, not at all.

What we're looking at when we talk about retention are trends over a series of years in comparison to local, state, and national averages. In theory, when a teacher or family is happy with where they are working, barring the personal circumstances listed above, they will continue working or learning at that school. As a leadership or data team, study the trends of your teacher and student retention, and examine whether the data lines up with your survey results on working conditions.

Having the right people in place is important as you continue to implement change, particularly in terms of teachers and staff. This may mean then that there is a higher displacement early in your culture shift as you figure out who is truly on board with the direction the school is heading. You ultimately need folks who will support the school mission and vision, share open and honest feedback, and build relationships with parents and students so that there are familiar faces year to year.

Eventually, change does happen over time. Individuals retire, may look to take on other professional roles, or have other life-changing moves. As we mentioned earlier, the test as to whether your efforts are a success is to see if they stick when those people are gone. Until then, continue to examine retention as *one* of the pieces for measuring the success for solving the climate and culture cube.

At Allen Jay, we recently had our first group of eighth-grade graduates. These students started with us in fifth grade and have spent 800 days in the school, through the good and tough times. We were proud to see that 90 percent of the students who started the school with us four years prior were graduating from Allen Jay. As we look ahead to the upcoming seventh and eighth-grade classes, those retention rates are even higher.

A DANGEROUS NUMBER

We believe surveys, attendance, behavior, and retention rates serve as valuable means for engaging in conversation about your school culture. They produce data discussions and anecdotal evidence for successes and areas of improvement. One number that can cause misrepresentation of culture, however, is standardized testing. Unfortunately, this type of data has become the most used source of conversation about schools because of its accessibility and publicity.

Although using test results to discuss teaching practices or rigor can be helpful to educators, a single multiple-choice test is not an indicator for the culture of a school (to be fair, none of the items we've talked about should be taken in singularity). Some people may argue that high test results may improve morale, and low scores may produce low morale. That is a slippery slope toward generalizations and inaccurate correlations.

Sometimes associated with test scores are school report cards—letter grades assigned to schools based on proficiency and growth of students on their

"Success is a science; if you have the conditions, you get the result."

OSCAR WILDE, IRISH POET AND PLAYWRIGHT

standardized tests. These grades are often public and shared in local media and online. While the "A" schools are often proudly celebrated, "D" and "F" schools are chastised by officials and labeled "failing schools." As a result, it is assumed that these schools must not be great places to send a child. What the public may not know is that there are many amazing schools across the country that are deemed "inadequate" by states.

Educating yourself on the true culture of a school is important. When possible, parents should visit a school before enrolling their children. Community members should take the time to get to know the school beyond the street address. If you really want to understand a school's culture, seek out stakeholders who are shining a limelight on their school. Listen to their stories, read what they have to say. Talk to students and teachers about their experiences; gather complete stories, not just a single account. And if you want to help people understand your school's culture, use your influence and skills to contribute to the betterment of your school's reputation. Find ways to help people look beyond a test score or letter grade to uncover the true success of the school.

WEBB ELEMENTARY

We both deeply respect and admire the work of Todd Nesloney, principal of Webb Elementary in Navasota, Texas, and author of *Kids Deserve It*. Todd works tirelessly for his students and staff. He also inspires hundreds of thousands of educators through his social media platforms and keynote speeches. We are fortunate to call him a friend.

As we were brainstorming the content for this chapter, a blog post that Todd wrote about his school popped into our heads. We chatted with him and asked if he would share his story for us again because it demonstrates the power culture has to remove old labels.

I still remember to this day, that moment that I first got the results for our campus from our state testing. It was the end of my first year as a principal, and I had been hired to take over an underperforming campus in Navasota, Texas. Everyone on the team worked tirelessly to pull ourselves out of an educational hole. We focused on the whole child—on growing every part of the students with whom we worked. It was a year filled with struggles but also a year where we felt like we had found great success. We weren't a perfect school by any means, but we had heart, and we fought hard for our kids.

When the results came back from that year, it was like a punch in the face. Our school was judged on four indexes. For the state to deem you successful, you have to meet their acceptable levels on three of the four indexes. When our results came back, we reached acceptable levels on one. Yes, just one. Now granted, we were very close on the other three, but it was devastating nonetheless. It felt like all the work we did that year was for nothing.

I remember sitting in that district administrator meeting, going over the results from each campus, and feeling utterly defeated when it came time to discuss my campus. Nowhere in those results did it discuss the great strides we had made with so many children. It didn't discuss the extra hours every staff member put in. It didn't discuss the before school tutoring, the Saturday school, the rides home when parents didn't show up, the food we bought for families ourselves, the cookouts we did at local apartments to build relationships—none of it. Those indicators simply didn't show that we were changing a culture.

On paper, it looked like another school that was doing the wrong things and needed to fix itself. And to those who aren't actually in the trenches in education, this one result from the state is sometimes all they care about.

I felt destroyed and confused. I couldn't believe we didn't rise to the state's levels of *acceptable.* And then I remembered a few things. First of all, I remembered that you can't change the entire course of a school in one year. Sometimes it takes a little longer. Even though I came into my first year with huge aspirations, I needed to be reminded that we couldn't fix everything right away. The second thing I remembered was I needed to not negate the value of all the great work we did—work that the test scores didn't reflect. There was an authentic culture shift happening at our school!

So many of the students we serve come from home lives we can't even imagine. Kids come to school carrying baggage that affects every aspect of their day. And yes, sometimes that baggage plays into how they perform on test day.

I am more than the scores. Our kids are *much* more than scores. Sure, I still wanted to raise the numbers; I wanted us out of the hole we were in. But I didn't want to create a place where the sole focus was raising scores. And that is a reminder I have to give myself daily. That I am more than my scores. That our campus is more than our scores. That we are investing in little lives and that, for years to come, they will remember what we do with them—how we make them feel.

We seek to grow the whole child at our campus. We seek to improve not only their educational lives but also their personal lives. Our goal is to grow them into educated citizens who care deeply, think creatively, problem-solve together, and seek to change the world. We are so much more than our scores.

Reflecting on Todd's story, you know what's going to "stick" for his students as they look back at their time at Webb Elementary? It's certainly not a day of testing. We are confident that his students will remember when their teachers cooked them hot dogs in their neighborhood or the car ride that Mr. Nesloney gave them when they didn't have any other way home. Culture starts and ends with the people in and around the school building. We have the power to make our school culture successful, and it requires each side of the cube to be in line with the next so that each stakeholder embodies the traits of a limitless school.

The road toward a successful
school culture is built with
bricks, and they're being laid
down one at a time.

ABE & ADAM

9

SET GOALS

A small group of academics, engineers, and math gurus discovered that it takes only twenty moves to solve a Rubik's Cube—no matter how jumbled the cube appears. This proven theory has become so popular in the world of Rubik's, the number twenty is now known as "God's Number" to cube enthusiasts.

It's time for the final piece of creating your limitless school. Setting short- and long-term goals, is necessary to launch you on your journey. Goals will pave the way to finding successes, identifying areas for growth, and measuring progress. Remember, it takes *time*! These goals are by no means exclusive, but they are starting blocks for stakeholders who are looking for ideas.

As a final ode to the Cube, in the pages that follow, we have outlined twenty goals for you to consider while building your limitless school. Your school-culture cube may require more or less than twenty moves to get the pieces into place, but when you finally see that your stakeholders are aligned, you will be on your way for a great ride because the limitless school knows no end!

1. MEASURE YOUR pH LEVEL

You may remember back in high school chemistry learning about pH levels, determining whether something is acidic or alkaline. We're not talking about that kind of pH here. This pH stands for Positive and Harmful, and refers to the number of positive versus harmful things that you say. As we discussed in the Integrity chapter, your words have meaning, and what you say (regardless of whether anyone hears your words) frames who you are. Measure the number of positive things you say to or about someone versus the number of harmful things. Set a goal to have your positive words outnumber your harmful ones. The limitless school supports and uplifts one another, and positive interactions and words are essential to its success.

2. FIND THE EARLY LEADERS

Change requires leadership. There are certain positions that involve leadership by definition: principal, superintendent, board of education member, PTA president, etc. These individuals on their own, however, cannot produce far-reaching change. They need other leaders to step forward and take on responsibilities. Like Lisa Burkhead did at Fertitta Middle School, you need to find the core individuals on the front end who can come together to brainstorm, plan, and execute early decisions that impact school culture. These people tend to be passionate and skilled but may not always step up unless given the opportunity. Principals, central office staff, and others in leadership positions need to identify these individuals and provide opportunity to join the movement.

3. Celebrate

As you begin your journey toward the limitless school, it will be easy to find things that don't go right: the effort that never picked up steam or the event that no one showed up to. It's easy to get bogged down with what isn't working. Set a goal to find at least one thing within the first month of solving your culture cube to celebrate. It may be an individual, an event, or an overall effort, but make sure that it highlights something positive. Continue to identify victories, small and large, that are recognized, and watch what happens to people's attitudes when it becomes the norm to find the things going well versus the things that aren't.

4. Find an Unlikely Partner

It's relatively easy to buddy up with someone who is in a position similar to yours. As a parent, it's simple working with another parent on a fundraiser or project. Board of education members will find it easy chatting with other board members about changing a district policy. The limitless school, however, requires many marriages, so set a goal to build your school culture by connecting with an unlikely partner. Teachers, find a community member to partner with on a class service project. Principals, find a parent with whom you can build a family-outreach program. Board of education members, elect a student representative to serve on your committees to hear a student's perspective on issues that affect them.

5. Identify Your Pillars

When starting the journey toward building or reframing school culture, it's easy to get caught up in a variety of initiatives and projects. Too many simultaneous movements can cause a traffic jam, and nothing ends up getting done. Step back and figure out what your essential pillars are for your school culture. Create pillars that everyone can recognize, recite, and embody. They should be present in every corner of the school, and anyone who enters the school should be able to see these pillars at work when they walk in. Communicate the pillars to all stakeholders so they become not just ideas, but words to live by.

6. STAY HUNGRY AND HUMBLE

It can be easy to get complacent as good things start happening at your school. You've earned a grant, won an award, or increased achievement. Things seem to be going your way, and you are soaking them in. And while you should certainly take time to enjoy and celebrate your accomplishments, it is imperative that you remain humble. Gloating or excessive celebration makes people turn away from you and your work. Remember, putting the pieces of the culture cube into place simply means that you're ready to take it to the next level! Stay hungry; the success of today can fade. The limitless school requires stakeholders to keep pushing to do what everyone else thinks can't be done.

7. LEAN TOWARD "YES"

To build a limitless school, you need to take risks. Risks may involve wacky ideas, strange requests, and far-reaching goals. Your gut reaction as a leader or decision-maker as these inquiries come across your table may be to immediately say "no." But stop and consider who is coming up with these ideas. More often than not, they are your most active teachers, enthusiastic parents, and creative students. Why would you want to immediately turn away and discourage your most engaged stakeholders? Leaning toward "yes" doesn't mean you agree or actually say "go ahead" with everything that is requested. That would be dangerous and ill-advised for any leader. But to "lean toward yes" means that when you hear an idea that you immediately want to shut down, ask more questions and learn about their vision. You may ultimately find a way to help that person make the idea (or a variation of it) happen. Building a habit of "leaning toward yes" creates a stronger community of listeners and mutual respect.

8. SEE WHAT OTHERS ARE DOING

We start teaching students about sharing from Pre-K on up. As educators, we should practice what we preach! Education should be a community of learners, and when we open our doors to others, we can all grow. As Allen Jay was being designed, Dr. Wheat went around to places like KIPP, Freedom Schools, the Ron Clark Academy, and other great schools to see what they were doing well. He said that Allen Jay was not going to be them, but that we were going to learn from what others were doing to devise our own path to success. To pay it forward, Allen Jay now opens its doors to others. When building your own school culture, don't be afraid to ask to visit other schools and see what they are doing. It is important to remember to enter schools with a reflective eye, not a critical one, so that you see how another school's practices can work for you.

9. JUST ASK

School budgets shrink a little each year. As resources decrease, schools are left to find new ways to bring innovation and engagement to the classrooms. There are many communities with rich resources (cultural, entrepreneurial, educational, etc.) that could serve as valuable assets to a school. Many of these resources, however, remain untapped, largely due to the fact that no one has asked them to help. It may be intimidating to go out and ask businesses, colleges, media, or professional associations for resources, but what's the worst they can say? No? If a fear of "no" is the only reason you haven't asked a community resource for help, make this one of your first goals! Before asking for money or material items, engage in conversation, make your *marriage* stronger, and see how you can help each other.

10. FEED THEM

As you are looking to attract stakeholders to the table, fancy posters, catchy slogans, and begging will only get you so far. In our experience, there is no greater way to get bottoms in seats than providing food. Ask any principal what events draw the most families. There is a good chance it will involve food. As you consider ways to bring food to your events and meetings, this provides an excellent opportunity to build relationships with local restaurants and caterers, who may serve as great resources and partners down the road.

11. OPEN HOUSES

Many of us recall open house as the time when summer officially ends, and you return to school to meet the teacher, find your classroom, and gather lots of papers to be filled out. We would like to expand this to an opportunity to welcome in guests of all kinds to see your school or building. Once or twice a year, open your doors to community members, families, central office personnel, or board of education officials to take a tour of your building, meet students and teachers, observe your classrooms, and learn about what the school is doing. Add a personal touch by creating invitations that cordially invite the individuals or groups to the event. When guests arrive, be ready to give great *impressions* so that they have a reason to share their positive experience with others. And, of course, have plenty of food! Open houses aren't exclusive to schools. Central offices, local businesses, and community centers should also find ways to mimic the concept of an open house so that all stakeholders play a role in building the culture of the school—and beyond.

12. POWER DOWN

We live in a day where we are connected to technology in every corner. From the phone to tablet to television and so on, we are never more than a few yards from some device that can answer a question, play a game, or produce a product. These devices are important and ingrained in our society, but they should not replace our ability to interact with another human face-to-face. Make it a goal to identify a designated part of your day where you can "power down" so you can interact with a fellow human without a device. Perhaps you have a meeting policy where no technology is permitted. Or maybe there is a bucket in the middle of the lunch table for all cell phones to go into (and you can play a game where the first person who touches their device pays for lunch!). Whatever your time is to power down, embrace it as a time to remain connected, just without a screen in front of you.

13. LAUGH

Laughter is the best medicine. In addition to being a catchy saying, science has proven that laughing actually does have health benefits. Laughter encourages others to smile and has been shown to keep couples together. Babies laugh before they can talk. Clearly, there's something powerful and natural about laughing, and we believe that laughter can help a school culture become stronger. Laughter is best when you form relationships with people whom you can laugh with (not at). Make it a goal to share fun moments and silly memories with each other. Laugh at yourself and let others laugh with you. Fill your limitless school with warm smiles and endearing laughter, making even the toughest days a bit lighter.

14. FIND YOUR HOOK

After your pillars have been established, set a goal to create your hook that takes your school mission and vision and turns it into something concrete. At Allen Jay, Morning Rally evolved as the hook to build lessons around character that molded the school culture. Through games, guest speakers, and opportunities to spend time with each other, stakeholders at Allen Jay found Morning Rally as the chance for students and staff to bring the school mission and vision to life in a fun and meaningful way. At the Ron Clark Academy, one hook came in the form of the coveted RCA letterman jacket. The jacket is earned by students who have demonstrated the values by which the school stands. Each faculty and staff member has to give a "yes" vote in order for the student to earn their jacket, a feat that can take multiple years! The culture of having to earn your jacket has created a greater sense of pride and celebration for the students once they do receive it.

15. FRESHEN UP

If school culture can be constructed, in part, from what you see, the aesthetics of a school should be discussed. If paint is chipping on the walls, if stairways have gum plastered to the railings, or if the school entrance has weeds and dead flowers, set a goal to freshen things up. Create a committee comprising staff members, parents, and students, or reach out to a local organization to volunteer to take on this task. As popular as the phrase "don't judge a book by its cover" remains, we know that it is human tendency to do just that. Be intentional and creative in your school's appearance. After the basics are taken care of, begin thinking of ways to add extras to the school through pictures of stakeholders in the hallways, banners celebrating school awards, or interesting artifacts or memorabilia.

16. BUILD CAPACITY

Your team is only as strong as your weakest link. Regardless of your position within or outside of a school, building people up is vital when you are trying to construct a positive school culture. Set goals to help others by sharing resources and making connections. Be quick to listen and deliberate in responding. Ask, "How can I help you?" before saying, "That won't work." Recognize others, even when you're being celebrated. When you have a school culture that aims to build capacity for those who have stake in it, the "blame game" that can engulf school culture shifts toward one that ensures each link is securely fastened to the next.

17. EVALUATE YOUR STAKEHOLDER RELATIONSHIPS

Teachers at the Ron Clark Academy take part in an activity at the beginning of each year that has teachers and staff put different color stickers next to the name of each child at the school, indicating how strong they feel their relationship is with that student (green = very strong, yellow = moderately strong, red = not strong). The stickers are tallied up at the end and the staff can see how certain kids do not have as strong a relationship with staff as others do. The staff then takes deliberate steps to strengthen relationships with those students throughout that year. A similar activity can be done with the various stakeholders of a school. Have parents evaluate relationships with teachers and administrators, students evaluate relationships with teachers, or central office staff evaluate relationships with their principals. This type of reflective activity allows stakeholder groups to identify potential areas of need for relationship building and steps to begin strengthening them.

18. MAKE MEMORIES AND MOMENTS

Our life is defined by moments and memories. The unforgettable trip you took, the game-winning goal you scored, your beautiful wedding. We naturally recall moments in our lives to measure successes and failures, joy and pain, fun and boredom. If we know that memories are such a powerful tool for the way we think about our lives, shouldn't we want to create positive moments for each other? We have that power! Providing a lesson that hooked the students, arranging an outing to a fancy restaurant, and getting tickets to a basketball game are just a few examples of ways that stakeholders can create lasting memories and moments. We have also met principals who slept on a roof after their students read enough books, athletes who came to a class and read to students, and superintendents who sat in a dunk tank or took pies to the face at the school fair. When we find ways to create positive memories and moments for each other, we contribute to building the culture for our limitless school.

19. BE CONSISTENT

We desire nothing more than for educators to take on the goals and ideas from this book to make positive changes to their school's culture. Further, we encourage you to build support by connecting with those who share your passion for improving your school. That said, we know it is natural for individuals to have personalized visions and agendas. Therefore, it is vital that individuals involved in making change for a common good discuss ways to be consistent in their approaches toward reform and improvements. As projects or initiatives begin, it is important to be on the same page so that decisions being made and steps being taken are in line with what is truly needed to make change. For example, if the school improvement team decides that it would like to move toward implementing Positive

Behavioral Interventions and Supports (PBIS) next year but leaves the conversation at that, the goal is left to everyone's different interpretations as to how it will be implemented. Will PBIS be used inside classrooms only at first or across the entire school? What are examples of expectations in the hallways, cafeteria, and buses? How will conversations with parents sound when they ask about PBIS? These types of important questions come only during conversations about how to be effective in implementing new initiatives. When consistent messaging is achieved, you will experience less frustration and confusion, and more cooperation and cohesion among all stakeholders.

20. START NOW

You've made it to the end of the twenty goals, but more importantly to the end of the book. We've inundated you with ideas, stories, and examples for ways to build your limitless school. It's a lot, and it may seem overwhelming, but our final goal for you is actually what we'd like you to do first: Start now! Don't worry if everything doesn't seem perfectly aligned just yet. And don't let naysayers or obstacles prevent you from kicking off your quest. Start now, and start simple. Don't take on everything at once, and certainly don't take it all on by yourself. Find some small and manageable shifts that you can make to show others that it really is possible to change your school's culture. You've gotta start somewhere. Slowly build your support system and network. Celebrate small victories and learn from failures. Keep your eyes open to opportunities, and put a smile on your face. Continue to twist and turn your cube to align your stakeholders! But most importantly, have fun as you build your limitless school.

Culture touches our hearts, our memories, and our souls. It connects us with one another and makes us a part of something meaningful. Building a limitless school culture cannot start without *you*.
Be the change you want to see.

ABE & ADAM

Keep the conversation going!

Follow @adamdovico and @abehege online, and tag #LimitlessSchool on social media to share what you're doing to create your own limitless school!

Create Your Limitless School! Bring Adam & Abe to Your Organization or Event

"THE LIMITLESS SCHOOL"

You've read the book, now bring the words to life! Abe and Adam, authors of *The Limitless School*, will bring the strategies and messages of how to solve the culture cube to you! Take part in an interactive experience that will leave you inspired and ready to make culture change!

"KIDS DESERVE A LIMITLESS SCHOOL"

Todd Nesloney, author of the acclaimed book *Kids Deserve It*, partners up with *The Limitless School* authors to bring administrators and school leaders the real-life experiences of how we each took our respective schools to new heights by building and changing culture!

Contact Ryan at ryan@premierespeakers.com for booking.

MORE FROM

DAVE BURGESS
Consulting, Inc.

Teach Like a PIRATE
Increase Student Engagement, Boost Your Creativity, and
Transform Your Life as an Educator
By Dave Burgess (@BurgessDave)

    Teach Like a PIRATE is the *New York Times'* best-selling book that has sparked a worldwide educational revolution. It is part inspirational manifesto that ignites passion for the profession and part practical road map, filled with dynamic strategies to dramatically increase student engagement. Translated into multiple languages, its message resonates with educators who want to design outrageously creative lessons and transform school into a life-changing experience for students.

Learn Like a PIRATE
Empower Your Students to Collaborate, Lead, and Succeed
By Paul Solarz (@PaulSolarz)

    Today's job market demands that students be prepared to take responsibility for their lives and careers. We do them a disservice if we teach them how to earn passing grades without equipping them to take charge of their education. In *Learn Like a PIRATE*, Paul Solarz explains how to design classroom experiences that encourage students to take risks and explore their passions in a stimulating, motivating, and supportive environment where improvement, rather than grades, is the focus. Discover how student-led classrooms help students thrive and develop into self-directed, confident citizens who are capable of making smart, responsible decisions all on their own.

P is for PIRATE
Inspirational ABC's for Educators
By Dave and Shelley Burgess (@Burgess_Shelley)

Teaching is an adventure that stretches the imagination and calls for creativity every day! In *P is for PIRATE*, husband and wife team Dave and Shelley Burgess encourage and inspire educators to make their classrooms fun and exciting places to learn. Tapping into years of personal experience and drawing on the insights of more than seventy educators, the authors offer a wealth of ideas for making learning and teaching more fulfilling than ever before.

Play Like a Pirate
Engage Students with Toys, Games, and Comics
By Quinn Rollins (@jedikermit)

Yes! School can be simultaneously fun and educational. In *Play Like a Pirate*, Quinn Rollins offers practical, engaging strategies and resources that make it easy to integrate fun into your curriculum. Regardless of the grade level you teach, you'll find inspiration and ideas that will help you engage your students in unforgettable ways.

eXPlore Like a Pirate
Gamification and Game-Inspired Course Design to Engage, Enrich, and Elevate Your Learners
By Michael Matera (@MrMatera)

Are you ready to transform your classroom into an experiential world that flourishes on collaboration and creativity? Then set sail with classroom game designer and educator Michael Matera as he reveals the possibilities and power of game-based learning. In *eXPlore Like a Pirate*, Matera serves as your experienced guide to help you apply the most motivational techniques of gameplay to your classroom. You'll learn gamification strategies that will work with and enhance (rather than replace) your current curriculum and discover how these engaging methods can be applied to any grade level or subject.

The Innovator's Mindset
Empower Learning, Unleash Talent, and Lead a Culture of Creativity
By George Couros (@gcouros)

The traditional system of education requires students to hold their questions and compliantly stick to the scheduled curriculum. But our job as educators is to provide new and better opportunities for our students. It's time to recognize that compliance doesn't foster innovation, encourage critical thinking, or inspire creativity—and those are the skills our students need to succeed. In *The Innovator's Mindset*, George Couros encourages teachers and administrators to empower their learners to wonder, to explore—and to become forward-thinking leaders.

Master the Media
How Teaching Media Literacy Can Save Our Plugged-in World
By Julie Smith (@julnilsmith)

Written to help teachers and parents educate the next generation, *Master the Media* explains the history, purpose, and messages behind the media. The point isn't to get kids to unplug; it's to help them make informed choices, understand the difference between truth and lies, and discern perception from reality. Critical thinking leads to smarter decisions—and it's why media literacy can save the world.

The Zen Teacher
Creating FOCUS, SIMPLICITY, and TRANQUILITY in the Classroom
By Dan Tricarico (@TheZenTeacher)

Teachers have incredible power to influence—even improve—the future. In *The Zen Teacher*, educator, blogger, and speaker Dan Tricarico provides practical, easy-to-use techniques to help teachers be their best—unrushed and fully focused—so they can maximize their performance and improve their quality of life. In this introductory guide, Dan Tricarico explains what it means to develop a Zen practice—something that has nothing to do with religion and everything to do with your ability to thrive in the classroom.

Lead Like a PIRATE
Make School Amazing for Your Students and Staff
By Shelley Burgess and Beth Houf
(@Burgess_Shelley, @BethHouf)

In *Lead Like a PIRATE*, education leaders Shelley Burgess and Beth Houf map out the character traits necessary to captain a school or district. You'll learn where to find the treasure that's already in your classrooms and schools—and how to bring out the very best in your educators. This book will equip and encourage you to be relentless in your quest to make school amazing for your students, staff, parents, and communities.

50 Things You Can Do with Google Classroom
By Alice Keeler and Libbi Miller
(@AliceKeeler, @MillerLibbi)

It can be challenging to add new technology to the classroom, but it's a must if students are going to be well-equipped for the future. Alice Keeler and Libbi Miller shorten the learning curve by providing a thorough overview of the Google Classroom App. Part of Google Apps for Education (GAfE), Google Classroom was specifically designed to help teachers save time by streamlining the process of going digital. Complete with screenshots, *50 Things You Can Do with Google Classroom* provides ideas and step-by-step instructions to help teachers implement this powerful tool.

50 Things to Go Further with Google Classroom
A Student-Centered Approach
By Alice Keeler and Libbi Miller
(@AliceKeeler, @MillerLibbi)

Today's technology empowers educators to move away from the traditional classroom where teachers lead and students work independently—each doing the same thing. In *50 Things to Go Further with Google Classroom: A Student-Centered Approach*, authors and educators Alice Keeler and Libbi Miller offer inspiration and resources to help you create a digitally rich, engaging, student-centered environment. They show you how to tap into the power of individualized learning that is possible with Google Classroom.

Pure Genius
Building a Culture of Innovation and Taking 20% Time to the Next Level
By Don Wettrick (@DonWettrick)

For far too long, schools have been bastions of boredom, killers of creativity, and way too comfortable with compliance and conformity. In *Pure Genius*, Don Wettrick explains how collaboration—with experts, students, and other educators—can help you create interesting, and even life-changing, opportunities for learning. Wettrick's book inspires and equips educators with a systematic blueprint for teaching innovation in any school.

140 Twitter Tips for Educators
Get Connected, Grow Your Professional Learning Network, and Reinvigorate Your Career
By Brad Currie, Billy Krakower, and Scott Rocco
(@bradmcurrie, @wkrakower, @ScottRRocco)

Whatever questions you have about education or about how you can be even better at your job, you'll find ideas, resources, and a vibrant network of professionals ready to help you on Twitter. In *140 Twitter Tips for Educators*, #Satchat hosts and founders of Evolving Educators, Brad Currie, Billy Krakower, and Scott Rocco, offer step-by-step instructions to help you master the basics of Twitter, build an online following, and become a Twitter rock star.

Ditch That Textbook
Free Your Teaching and Revolutionize Your Classroom
By Matt Miller (@jmattmiller)

Textbooks are symbols of centuries-old education. They're often outdated as soon as they hit students' desks. It's time to ditch those textbooks—and those textbook assumptions about learning! In *Ditch That Textbook*, teacher and blogger Matt Miller encourages educators to throw out meaningless, pedestrian teaching and learning practices. He empowers them to evolve and improve on old, standard teaching methods. *Ditch That Textbook* is a support system, toolbox, and manifesto to help educators free their teaching and revolutionize their classrooms.

How Much Water Do We Have?
5 Success Principles for Conquering Any Challenge and Thriving in Times of Change
By Pete Nunweiler with Kris Nunweiler

In *How Much Water Do We Have?* Pete Nunweiler identifies five key elements—information, planning, motivation, support, and leadership—that are necessary for the success of any goal, life transition, or challenge. Referring to these elements as the 5 Waters of Success, Pete explains that, like the water we drink, you need them to thrive in today's rapidly paced world. If you're feeling stressed out, overwhelmed, or uncertain at work or at home, pause and look for the signs of dehydration. Learn how to find, acquire, and use the 5 Waters of Success—so you can share them with your team and family members.

Instant Relevance
Using Today's Experiences to Teach Tomorrow's Lessons
By Denis Sheeran (@MathDenisNJ)

Every day, students in schools around the world ask the question, "When am I ever going to use this in real life?" In *Instant Relevance*, author and keynote speaker Denis Sheeran equips you to create engaging lessons *from* experiences and events that matter to your students. Learn how to help your students see meaningful connections between the real world and what they learn in the classroom—because that's when learning sticks.

The Classroom Chef
Sharpen Your Lessons. Season Your Classes.
Make Math Meaningful.
By John Stevens and Matt Vaudrey
(@Jstevens009, @MrVaudrey)

Math teachers and instructional coaches John Stevens and Matt Vaudrey share their secret recipes, ingredients, and tips for serving up lessons that engage students and help them "get" math. You can use these ideas and methods as-is, or better yet, tweak them and create your own enticing educational meals. The message the authors share is that, with imagination and preparation, every teacher can be a classroom chef.

Start. Right. Now.
Teach and Lead for Excellence
By Todd Whitaker, Jeff Zoul, and Jimmy Casas
(@ToddWhitaker, @Jeff_Zoul, @casas_jimmy)

In their work leading up to *Start. Right. Now.*, Todd Whitaker, Jeff Zoul, and Jimmy Casas studied educators from across the nation and discovered four key behaviors of excellence: Excellent leaders and teachers *Know the Way, Show the Way, Go the Way, and Grow Each Day.* If you are ready to take the first step toward excellence, this motivating book will put you on the right path.

The Writing on the Classroom Wall
How Posting Your Most Passionate Beliefs about Education Can Empower Your Students, Propel Your Growth, and Lead to a Lifetime of Learning
By Steve Wyborney (@SteveWyborney)

In *The Writing on the Classroom Wall*, Steve Wyborney explains how posting and discussing Big Ideas can lead to deeper learning. You'll learn why sharing your ideas will sharpen and refine them. You'll also be encouraged to know that the Big Ideas you share don't have to be profound to make a profound impact on learning. In fact, Steve explains, it's okay if some of your ideas fall *off* the wall. What matters most is sharing them.

LAUNCH
Using Design Thinking to Boost Creativity and Bring Out the Maker in Every Student
By John Spencer and A.J. Juliani
(@spencerideas, @ajjuliani)

Something happens in students when they define themselves as *makers* and *inventors* and *creators*. They discover powerful skills—problem-solving, critical thinking, and imagination—that will help them shape the world's future—*our* future. In LAUNCH, John Spencer and A.J. Juliani provide a process that can be incorporated into every class at every grade level, even if you don't consider yourself a "creative teacher." And if you dare to innovate and view creativity as an essential skill, you will empower your students to change the world—starting right now.

Kids Deserve It!
Pushing Boundaries and Challenging Conventional Thinking
By Todd Nesloney and Adam Welcome
(@TechNinjaTodd, @awelcome)

In *Kids Deserve It!*, Todd and Adam encourage you to think big and make learning fun and meaningful for students. Their high-tech, high-touch, and highly engaging practices will inspire you to take risks, shake up the status quo, and be a champion for your students. While you're at it, you just might rediscover why you became an educator in the first place.

Escaping the School Leader's Dunk Tank
How to Prevail When Others Want to See You Drown
By Rebecca Coda and Rick Jetter
(@RebeccaCoda, @RickJetter)

No school leader is immune to the effects of discrimination, bad politics, revenge, or ego-driven coworkers. These kinds of dunk-tank situations can make an educator's life miserable. By sharing real-life stories and insightful research, the authors (who are dunk-tank survivors themselves) equip school leaders with the practical knowledge and emotional tools necessary to survive and, better yet, avoid getting "dunked."

Teaching Math with Google Apps
50 G Suite Activities
By Alice Keeler and Diana Herrington
(@AliceKeeler, @mathdiana)

Google Apps give teachers the opportunity to interact with students in a more meaningful way than ever before, while G Suite empowers students to be creative, critical thinkers who collaborate as they explore and learn. In *Teaching Math with Google Apps*, educators Alice Keeler and Diana Herrington demonstrate fifty different ways to bring math classes to the twenty-first century with easy-to-use technology.

Your School Rocks . . . So Tell People!
Passionately Pitch and Promote the Positives Happening on Your Campus
By Ryan McLane and Eric Lowe
(@McLane_Ryan, @EricLowe21)

Great things are happening in your school every day. The problem is, no one beyond your school walls knows about them. School principals Ryan McLane and Eric Lowe offer more than seventy immediately action-able tips along with easy-to-follow instructions and links to video tutorials to help you get the word out. This practical guide will equip you to create an effective and manageable communication strategy using social media tools. Learn how to keep your students' families and community connected, informed, and excited about what's going on in your school.

Table Talk Math
A Practical Guide for Bringing Math into Everyday Conversations
By John Stevens (@Jstevens009)

Making math part of families' everyday conversa-tions is a powerful way to help children and teens learn to love math. In *Table Talk Math*, John Stevens offers par-ents (and teachers!) ideas for initiating authentic, math-based conversations that will get kids to notice and be curious about all the numbers, patterns, and equations in the world around them.

Shattering the Perfect Teacher Myth
6 Truths That Will Help You THRIVE as an Educator
By Aaron Hogan (@aaron_hogan)

The idyllic myth of the perfect teacher perpetuates unrealistic expectations that erode self-confidence and set teachers up for failure. Author and educator Aaron Hogan is on a mission to shatter the myth of the perfect teacher by equipping educators with strategies that help them shift out of survival mode and THRIVE.

Shift This!
How to Implement Gradual Changes for MASSIVE Impact in Your Classroom
By Joy Kirr (@JoyKirr)

Establishing a student-led culture that isn't focused on grades and homework but on individual responsibility and personalized learning may seem like a daunting task—especially if you think you have to do it all at once. But significant change is possible, sustainable, and even easy when it happens little by little. In *Shift This!*, educator and speaker Joy Kirr explains how to make gradual shifts—in your thinking, teaching, and approach to classroom design—that will have a massive impact in your classroom. Make the first shift today!

Unmapped Potential
An Educator's Guide to Lasting Change
By Julie Hasson and Missy Lennard (@PPrincipals)

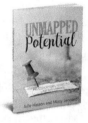

No matter where you are in your educational career, chances are you have, at times, felt overwhelmed and overworked. Maybe you feel that way right now. If so, you aren't alone. But the more important news is that things can get better! You simply need the right map to guide you from frustrated to fulfilled. *Unmapped Potential* offers advice and practical strategies to help you find your unique path to becoming the kind of educator—the kind of person—you want to be.

Social LEADia
Moving Students from Digital Citizenship to Digital Leadership
By Jennifer Casa-Todd (@JCasaTodd)

Equipping students for their future begins by helping them become digital leaders now. In our networked society, students need to learn how to leverage social media to connect to people, passions, and opportunities to grow and make a difference. *Social LEADia* addresses the need to shift the conversations at school and at home from digital citizenship to digital leadership.

Spark Learning
3 Keys to Embracing the Power of Student Curiosity
By Ramsey Musallam (@ramusallam)

Inspired by his popular TED Talk "3 Rules to Spark Learning," this book combines brain science research, proven teaching methods, and Ramsey's personal story to empower you to improve your students' learning experiences by inspiring inquiry and harnessing its benefits. If you want to engage students in more interesting and effective learning, this is the book for you.

Ditch That Homework
Practical Strategies to Help Make Homework Obsolete
By Matt Miller and Alice Keeler
(@jmattmiller, @alicekeeler)

In *Ditch That Homework*, Matt Miller and Alice Keeler discuss the pros and cons of homework, why teachers assign it, and what life could look like without it. As they evaluate the research and share parent and teacher insights, the authors offer a convincing case for ditching homework and replacing it with more effective and personalized learning methods.

The Four O'Clock Faculty
A Rogue Guide to Revolutionizing Professional Development
By Rich Czyz (@RACzyz)

Author Rich Czyz is on a mission to revolutionize professional learning for all educators. In *The Four O'Clock Faculty*, Rich identifies ways to make PD meaningful, efficient, and, above all, personally relevant. This book is a practical guide that reveals why some PD is so awful and what you can do to change the model for the betterment of you and your colleagues.

Culturize
Every Student. Every Day. Whatever It Takes.
By Jimmy Casas (@casas_jimmy)

In *Culturize*, author and education leader Jimmy Casas shares insights into what it takes to cultivate a community of learners who embody the innately human traits our world desperately needs. His stories reveal how these "soft skills" can be honed while meeting and exceeding academic standards of twenty-first-century learning.

Code Breaker
Increase Creativity, Remix Assessment, and Develop a Class of Coder Ninjas!
By Brian Aspinall (@mraspinall)

Code Breaker equips you to use coding in your classroom to turn curriculum expectations into skills. Students learn how to identify problems, develop solutions, and use computational thinking to apply and demonstrate their learning. Best of all, you don't have to be a "computer geek" to empower your students with these essential skills.

The Wild Card
7 Steps to an Educator's Creative Breakthrough
By Hope and Wade King
(@hopekingteach, @wadeking7)

Have you ever wished you were more creative . . . or that your students were more engaged in your lessons? *The Wild Card* is your step-by-step guide to experiencing a creative breakthrough in your classroom with your students. Wade and Hope King show you how to draw on your authentic self to deliver your content creatively and be the wild card who changes the game for your learners.

Stories from Webb
The Ideas, Passions, and Convictions of a Principal and His School Family
By Todd Nesloney (@TechNinjaTodd)

Stories from Webb goes right to the heart of education. Told by award-winning principal Todd Nesloney and his dedicated team of staff and teachers at Webb Elementary, this book will remind you why you became an educator. You'll be reinvigorated by these relatable stories—and you just may be inspired to tell your own!

About the Authors

Abe Hege has been a middle school teacher, dean of students, coach, district presenter, and currently serves as an assistant principal. Abe has a passion for school culture, character education, and above all else, students. Living by the motto, "In one encounter, you can change someone's life forever," Abe uses humor, motivation, and a little dose of luck to reach students, teachers, community members, district officials, and anyone else that will lend an ear. Abe is married to his beautiful wife, Brittany, and they have one son, Jeremiah.

Adam Dovico is an accomplished teacher, principal, college professor, author, and speaker who has spent his career working with schools and educators across the country on building school culture, engaging students, and figuring out what educators *can* do for kids! His unique stories combined with his wacky costumes, sense of humor, and practical ideas have made him a favorite among kids and adults of all ages! Adam is married to his wife, Jaclyn, and they have two sons, Ryder and Maddox.